Greatness Unleashed

Inspire. Inform. Instruct. Impact.

DeAndre M. Riley

Cover Design: Lee Graphix PR and Design Group
Interior Design: Antoine D. Jackson of Sow Graphics & Publications, LLC
Edited by Tenita C. Johnson of So It Is Written, LLC
Author Photography: Stephen D. Crosson of Crosseyed Photography

All scripture quotations are taken from the King James Version of the Bible, unless otherwise noted. Copyright © 1977, 1984, 2991 by Thomas Nelson, Inc. and from The Message. Copyright © 1993, 1994, 1995, 1996, 2000, 2001, 2002. Used by permission of NavPress Publishing Group

Printed in the United States of America

DEDICATION

I dedicate this book to my grandparents, Dave and Ophelia
Walker. I would have never discovered the greatness within
without your guidance.
To my wife, Porsha: You have shown me that nothing is
impossible. I love you.
To the memory of Michael and Anita Riley, my birth parents: I
often wish you were here to see the man that I have become.

CONTENTS

Greatness Unleashed
A Poem by Danita Crosson

It started off as a seed.

With a spark, it started to breathe.

A taste of responsibility caused it to feed.

The seed of faith grew action and up sprung belief.

The power of vision is what caused me to see,

That with limitless potential, so much can be achieved.

Though most people thought I was only chasing a dream,

They hadn't been shown the things I'd seen.

Their doubt didn't stop me.

Perseverance saved me.

My attitude determined where God placed me.

A change was to come.

I adapted graciously.

I had been called into service and instructed to lead.

Inspired by relationships throughout my journey,

I looked forward to where I would soon be.

The impact of influence would guide my feet.

God would equip me with the tools I'd need.

I had strength to conquer the obstacles I'd meet.

It was time for my greatness to be unleashed.

Introduction

"There is greatness within you!" These are some of the most life-changing words that I have ever heard. These are the words of author, speaker and world-renowned entrepreneur, Les Brown. One day, I received a link to a video by Les Brown entitled, *"The Mindset of the Entrepreneur."* There he echoed those five simple words. He explained in the video that although there was greatness within him, there was a time when he hadn't realized it. It was as if he was talking to me directly. I can't explain the feeling I had while he described that we all have a purpose that must be realized. For me it was confirmation.

From that moment, I knew that my life had a greater purpose than that which I had tapped into. Since that day, I measure the worth of my life by the amount of people I can help discover the greatness that lies within them. Greatness isn't out of reach. It truly lies within us all. Greatness is a direct result of a fulfilled call and ongoing utilization of gifts.

Before seeing the video by Les Brown, Daniel Grandberry, who is my pastor, spoke a few words that I will never forget. While sitting in the pulpit at Gordy Memorial Church, Pastor Grandberry challenged the congregation to utilize the gifts that God has given them. He explained that there are many people who underutilize their gifts. He mentioned that many people sit on their gifts due to what they perceive to be a lack of opportunity.

I was one of those people. I was the person who sat on my gift because I didn't feel as if there was a platform for me. I knew that I had the gift to speak. Furthermore, I recognized that God called me to be a preacher and minister. However, I only limited my gift and call to the opportunities that presented themselves in the church. Therefore, if the opportunity didn't present itself in the church, my gifts went unused. After hearing Pastor Grandberry's message, I sought to utilize my gift in a greater capacity.

It all started with my cell phone. I recorded inspirational videos and posted them on social media sites. Since that time, I've become a talk show radio host, where I exclaim, "I've Got Something to Say." In addition, I've hosted a television show, conferences, events and workshops. I am both an entrepreneur and author. Essentially, I have unleashed my greatness to the world. My purpose and call is more clearly defined, and my reach has expanded. It is my hope that through reading this book, you too will discover and unleash your greatness.

What Is Greatness?

Greatness has nothing to do with your status in society, your family tree, your educational level or your income. Greatness is unleashed by maximizing the gifts, talents and skills that God has planted inside you. It is being successful in fulfilling your God-given purpose. Greatness is being the best *you* that you can possibly be. It is using what you have been given to make an impact in the lives of those in this world.

More than likely, there is at least one person that has impacted your life in a great way. This person may not be wealthy or educated, and they may not have even contributed to the technological advances of our day. However, this person is a hard worker, a person of integrity, and one who loves

> *Greatness is unleashed by maximizing the gifts, talents and skills that God has planted inside you.*

and takes care of their family. He or she is faithful and committed to their friends. This person is also full of wisdom. Whether or not this person meets the standards for success according to society, you consider this person to be one of the greatest people that you know.

Author Scott Adams said the people in his life weren't even aware of the influence that they had in his life. Perhaps he's referring to teachers, coaches, neighbors or family members. Perhaps none of them came close to accomplishing the things that he has. But that doesn't mean they can't be great. You can be great within the ability and gifting that you have been given.

Why Greatness Unleashed?

While there are countless books flooding the market that speak to the subject of greatness, few, if any, approach greatness from this perspective. Many books about greatness focus on what you as an individual can gain instead of what you can do to empower others. Furthermore, while I do utilize some examples of societal greats, I don't use these examples to make their lives and accomplishments into rules that you must live by. Many books on greatness focus on what others have accomplished and use that as the sole basis on how you too can become great. Nothing is wrong with that. However, the mention of historical, successful and influential people in this piece is used solely to help you see that greatness is for us all. It is my prayer that through these examples you will grow in faith and be inspired to be great.

You will accomplish the following:

1. Recognize that we all have the ability to be great. Regardless of who you are, your income level, or your family background, greatness is within you.

2. Greatness is best realized when you endeavor to serve and empower others to live the lives that they were destined to

live. *"If you aren't making a difference in someone else's life other than yours, you are wasting your life."* I couldn't agree more. You can't be great unless you impact the lives of others to be great.

3. In accomplishing the first two goals, you will be able to live life with purpose, prosperity, joy and peace. All that we ever hope to become and accomplish comes as a result of unleashing the greatness that is within us.

This book will help you understand that we all possess seeds of greatness. Moreover, this book will serve as an outline to help you discover the power to unleash the greatness within. Found throughout the pages of this book are principles—learned from personal experience, the lifestyles and accomplishments of others, and principles from my favorite book, the Bible. These principles will help you tap into your greatness and serve as the driving force to help you live the life that you were destined to live. By applying these principles, you will discover the power to unleash the greatness within. Greatness is a quality that exists within us all; never forget that. I challenge you to embrace this idea as you read. You will discover this truth and begin to live a life with fuller purpose and power.

I titled the book *Greatness Unleashed*; not *Greatness Revealed, Greatness Unlocked* or *Greatness Discovered*. While I want you to discover, uncover and even unlock the greatness within, I want you to take it a step further and unleash it.

Unleashed, as defined by Webster's dictionary, means to free or let loose. It is also defined as allowing something powerful to happen. Once you discover your greatness, put it into motion. Make full use of your greatness. Make something powerful happen. Let go of any hindrances to your greatness. Break free from fear, doubt and defeat. Greatness is within you. But, it's up to you to unleash it!

Lastly, as you are reading this book remember these four words—*Inspire, Inform, Instruct, Impact.* I want you to gain inspiration, information, and instruction from this piece; all with the hope that your life will be impacted in a great way. Moreover, I want you to seek how you can do the same in the lives of those in this world. Utilizing your greatness in this matter is truly unleashing it to the world.

1

THE POWER OF AWARENESS
RECOGNIZING THE GREATNESS WITHIN

"What is necessary to change a person is to change his awareness of himself. – Abraham Maslow

When we tap into our gifts and talents, they propel us into the realm of the extraordinary. These gifts and talents have the ability to take us from mere existence to greatness. The key is that we must tap into the potential that we have and awaken those possibilities that lie dormant inside.

Unfortunately, many people are completely oblivious to the greatness that lies within them. Even those who may have recognized their gifts and talents are sometimes leery and doubtful about the value they hold. Countless individuals never realize their greatness. It is my personal endeavor to help decrease the number of people who have yet to tap into their unlimited potential, helping them realize that they are more powerful than what meets the eye.

I was once fearful and full of doubt. I lacked the discipline necessary to uncover and unleash my greatness. My life was unfulfilling and seemed to be a total waste. I searched constantly for my purpose. I thought I could find it in a job. Maybe my purpose was in a relationship. Perhaps my greatness was connected to a degree or a title, I thought. But none of these proved to unlock the mystery to my purpose.

Don't get me wrong. I am not saying that, in some cases, these things can't and won't influence me. Nor am I saying that your greatness won't be enhanced or accompanied by some of the aforementioned things. However, we have to use the gifts and talents that God put in us at birth if we are going to experience the

> *It won't be until we have discovered the power of our gifts that we will discover our purpose and unleash the greatness within.*

abundant prosperity and joy we desire. Unless we unleash our greatness, and tap into our potential, we will never become what God has called us to be. Nor will we be effective in making an impact.

We were all placed here to make a difference. Within us lies the ability to leave a mark so impressionable that, without a doubt, the world would know that you lived. Therefore, we should seek to make the most of the time and gifts that we have been afforded. We should seek to discover how we can use our gifts to make a difference. We must find our life's worth. It won't be until we have discovered the power of our gifts that we will discover our purpose and unleash the greatness within.

I haven't always been a preacher and a speaker. Nor have I always had the desire to be. However, before I was born, it was predestined for me to preach and speak. I just wasn't aware of it. When I answered the call from God to preach, I was forced to search myself in a way that I hadn't done prior to the call. The one thing I had constantly tried to avoid my whole life was placed right in my face—my fear of public speaking. I realized that if I was going to be an effective ambassador for God, I had to overcome that fear and improve my public speaking ability. I made a decision to overcome that fear and trust God, seeking to utilize the gifts that he placed within me.

Once I identified my gift, speaking and preaching grew easier and easier, and more and more enjoyable. Moreover, my confidence increased and I became more convinced of my purpose. Today, no one has to coerce, convince or pressure me to speak. In fact, I now seek the opportunity to speak every chance I can. It is a love and passion that I've discovered, and it is all connected to my purpose and gift.

I now recognize that the gifts within me had been lying dormant all the while. Had I never discovered my gift, I would have never discovered my purpose. Had I never discovered my purpose, I would have never unleashed the greatness within.

Now it's up to you to discover your purpose. I found it in seeking the one who created me. I would start there. Secondly,

> *God created us all with a purpose, and since He is the creator, He understands what our lives should reflect.*

determine what you are good at and what you love to do. Finally, figure out how you can use that desire and passion to make a difference. In doing so, you will unleash the greatness within.

Back To The Basics

What do you want out of life? Secondly, and more importantly, what does God want out of your life? Do the two correlate? A life with no defined purpose is a life wasted. God created us all with a purpose, and since He is the creator, He understands what our lives should reflect.

God has given us the responsibility to care for, love and serve others. It's key that you have a defined plan as to how you will carry out your divine purpose. For some, the assignment is to speak, preach or teach. Others are called to act, sing or become a musician. Maybe you're the next media tycoon, politician or major developer. Regardless of what your assignment is, you must identify your life's worth and make the most of what you have been given.

In the book of Matthew, the Bible recounts Jesus' parable of the talents. This story when translated, explains how we are given gifts and talents according to our own separate abilities. Furthermore, this story impresses upon us the necessity to make full use of the talents God has dealt to us. This parable conveys the reward of using the talents given to you, as well as the consequences in not doing so. There were three servants entrusted as stewards over their talents, yet only two increased what they had.

The assignments that God has given us are more than within reach of our abilities. God will never require more from you

When our gifts and talents are mixed with our various passions, it often leads us directly to our calling.

than what you are able to produce. Moreover, the gifts that He has blessed us with are what will enable us to carry out that assignment. Therefore, if we are called to it, we are more than capable of answering and carrying out that call. You must understand that we all have a purpose and reason for living. As you examine yourself, think about your call and purpose. If you are unsure, seek to find out your specific purpose. When we search deep within ourselves, we will find clear passion and the purpose that God has given for our lives. When our gifts and talents are mixed with our various passions, it often leads us directly to our calling. Recognizing your call and purpose in life is vital in unleashing the greatness within.

Have you pursued your call and passion? Have you maximized your gifts and talents? If not, why haven't you? You can't escape the responsibility of your call. You must answer the call if you are going to reach your full potential, realize your dreams and unleash the greatness within you. Moreover, our health, wealth and prosperity are all interconnected to the fulfillment of our required assignment and purpose.

Much like the parable of the talents, you can choose to take what you have and multiply it to bring forth increase, or you can choose to be like the one

> *If you're not walking in your purpose and calling, you are like a plant that doesn't receive ample water and sunlight. Eventually, it will no longer serve its intended purpose and it will wither away.*

servant that decided he would hide his talent and do nothing with it. This mentality will not only cause you to lose out on all that God has for you, but even that which you have now will be stripped away from you. If you're not walking in your purpose and calling, you are like a plant that doesn't receive ample water and sunlight. Eventually, it will no longer serve its intended purpose and it will wither away.

What Makes Them Different?

Consider the lifestyles and accomplishments of the many greats in our society. When you think about individuals like Bill Gates, Oprah Winfrey, Steve Jobs, Michael Jordan, Muhammad Ali and President Barack Obama, to name a few, what is it about these individuals that has allowed them to experience the amount of success that they have? Are they any different than you and me?

Many individuals possess the same gifts and talents that the people I mentioned possess, yet they are barely

> *...greatness was not reserved for a select few. Greatness is available to us all.*

making it. Despite having the ability to be great, many struggle with accepting this truth. Certainly, greatness was not reserved for a select few. Greatness is available to us all.

The sad reality is that millions have gifts, ideas and passions, yet these things remain dormant and eventually die. Oprah may not be the best talk show host. Steve Jobs may not have been the most technologically inclined. Michael Jordan may not have had the best jump shot in the NBA. However, one thing is synonymous of all the greats—the desire to achieve their purpose. Instead of allowing their gifts to remain idle and unused, they put forth the effort to achieve greatness.

These people are great examples of those who have unleashed their greatness in an attempt to make an impact in this world.

Furthermore, there are many others like them who have recognized that in order to be great, certain behaviors should be practiced, and one should possess certain traits. They didn't do anything special. They simply mastered basic principles that helped them to make the most of their gifts, callings and opportunities.

Therefore, let it be understood that we all possess the power to unleash the greatness within. Found within the pages of this book are principles that will help you to do just that. In addition, this book will serve as a reminder to anyone who may have already tapped into their greatness, but needs the encouragement to sustain success. Whether you are young or old, rich or poor, educated or not, apply the principles within this book to kick start the journey toward unleashing the greatness within.

FINAL THOUGHT

No one is prohibited from living a life of greatness. We simply have to be aware of this possibility. Identify all of the areas in your life that will contribute to the greatness within. Once you have done this, you will be certain to unleash your greatness to the world.

2

THE POWER OF RESPONSIBILTY
IT ALL BEGINS WITH YOU

"The price of greatness is responsibility" – Winston Churchill

Let today be the day that all excuses die. Allow today to be the day that you take full accountability for your life, deeds, actions and mistakes. While it can be real easy to blame others for your shortcomings and failures, decide that no longer will you play the blame game. It's time to embrace the fact that any amount of success available to you begins by taking the necessary steps to secure that success. Therefore, decide today that you are going to be great. Decide today that you will experience God's best for your life, despite the opposing forces that may confront you.

Unleashing your greatness requires you to be responsible for your life. Those who are great are those who have become accountable in all areas of their life. Greatness can only be realized by you. No one can be responsible for you being great. It all begins with you.

THE VICTIM MENTALITY

Too often in society, people blame others for their lack of success, opportunities and advancements. If you log onto Facebook or Twitter on any given day, you will find countless individuals ranting about what is *not* right in their lives. They seem to gain some sort of euphoric feeling from venting their displeasure with life, society, and those around them. They succumb to the victim mentality and try to convince themselves that others are to blame for their shortcomings. People blame unemployment. They blame the educational systems. Some blame their upbringing and the influences of society for the reason why they haven't measured up to the level of success they desire. What these individuals fail to realize is that no one is to blame for their quality of life but them, and them alone.

I am, in no way, diminishing the struggles and obstacles that you may be facing. But I want you to realize that we all have issues and situations that arise in our lives that are meant for our demise. We all have circumstances and stormy weather that confronts us. Sometimes, life is just outright difficult, making success appear unattainable. But like it is often said, *"if success were in fact easy, everyone would be successful."*

If "making it" was a walk in the park, we would all be living large, but the truth remains that struggles are eminent. Job said, *"Man that is born of a woman is of few days, and full of trouble"* (Job 14:1 ASV). But I am reminded of the words of James, *"Dear brothers and sisters, when troubles come your way, consider it an opportunity for great joy. For you know that when your faith is tested, your endurance is fully developed, you will be perfect and complete, needing nothing"* (James 1:2-4 NLT).

Struggles in life are only present to strengthen you. The bitter taste of defeat that you sometimes experience will soon be replaced with the sweet taste of victory if you continue to

{ *Struggles in life are only present to strengthen you.* }

fight. You must recognize and label your struggles for what they are. Understand that everything that goes wrong is not an indicator of failure. Bad things happen and unpleasant days are inevitable. But don't allow them to cause you to become the victim. Do your best to allow those unfortunate events to develop you.

Be Accountable

Those with the victim mentality often give way to the belief that hard times are indicative of failure. Furthermore, they take the stance that every person that doesn't agree with their goals or plans is an enemy. This simply isn't the case. Sometimes, God allows you to endure certain hardships so that you will be equipped to handle the success that is coming your way. The hardships I've experienced helped shape me. In addition, many that I once considered to be enemies were actually those who God put in place to help elevate me to the next level.

Growing up, I was very rebellious and contentious. I always challenged authority and blamed others for my failures. I was rude and disrespectful; thus, I was unteachable and stubborn. As I grew older, certain individuals challenged my behavior. They told me when I was wrong and corrected me, whether I liked it or not.

Elder Randall Greenwood, who is now the pastor of Bailey Temple COGIC, was one of those people. As a young man, I thought Elder Greenwood had it out for me. It seemed like whatever I did, he always had something to say, and I always perceived his commentary as negative. One day, I let my anger get the best of me, and I blew up at him. God later revealed to me that all along, Elder Greenwood had simply been trying to help me. He recognized that certain traits and qualities in me were hidden by my dysfunctional behavior, and he was simply trying to uncover the greatness within me. It is because of people like Randall Greenwood that I am the man I am today.

It wasn't until I stopped playing the victim that I realized I am responsible for my life and actions. Until we own who we are and bring our negative behaviors under subjection, we will continue to play the victim in our minds, all while missing out on the chance to become great. Often people believe that if they blame others for their shortcomings it will somehow change the outcome. However, playing the victim or blaming others does not negate the consequences that come with us not doing what we know to do.

God told Adam that he had access to every tree in the Garden of Eden, except one. For some reason, that wasn't sufficient enough for Adam. He soon ate from the tree that God had commanded him *not* to eat from. Once Adam took a bite of the fruit from the forbidden tree, he tried to offset the responsibility when it came time for punishment. *"It was the woman you gave me,"* Adam argued. Maybe He thought the

> *Until we own who we are and bring our negative behaviors under subjection, we will continue to play the victim in our minds, all while missing out on the chance to become great.*

Lord would forgive his actions because of peer pressure. Adam had to accept the consequences of his actions.

God has given us access to so much in this life. Like Adam, there are opportunities, blessings and favor that awaits us; however, we are still faced with the responsibility to act in a manner that will warrant us receiving all that life has to offer us. We cannot expect to make poor decisions and still believe that we will receive the rewards that only come as a result of good decision making. Nor can we blame others when things don't go as we planned. We must be accountable and responsible for our actions.

THE VICTOR MENTALITY

No matter how much a person gives to you, or how much they may want you to succeed, you must want it for yourself. No matter how much a person pushes you, walks with you, or provides you with opportunities, you have to want it for yourself. No one can get the grades for you. No one can interview for that job for you. No one can advance in the company for you. You have to put in the work necessary to gain what you desire.

It all begins with you. Ralph Waldo Emerson said, "No one can bring you peace but yourself." Decide

> *If you want peace, pursue it. If you want love, give it. If you want opportunity, create it.*

what you want and position yourself to receive what you desire. If you want peace, pursue it. If you want love, give it. If you want opportunity, create it. George Bernard Shaw said, "Those who make it in this life are those who look for the opportunities that they want. When they can't find them, they create them." Keep looking for what you want in life, and when you can't find it, create the opportunity and the atmosphere that is conducive to receive what you are seeking.

In order for you to receive certain things, the environment has to be right. You can't expect oranges to grow in the dead of winter. You can't expect to receive a scholarship with bad grades. Nor is it likely for you to receive a promotion with a poor work ethic. You must put the work in, while applying the proper techniques, to achieve the success you covet.

Think about professional athletes. Kobe Bryant, for example, didn't wait until he got to the NBA to become a good basketball player. He didn't become great after he won the championship rings and MVP awards. But it was the greatness within that got him to where he is today. Long before his success, he exhibited the behaviors that were conducive to him excelling. Individuals like Kobe Bryant teach us that you must tap into your greatness and resemble what you want before you can have it. Your life must reflect the success that you desire.

If, and when, we tap into our greatness, we will experience a quality of life that will supersede our own imaginations. However, unlocking this greatness requires a shift of focus from feeling victimized and defeated to believing that we are victors and more than conquerors. The difference between the successful and the one who isn't is simply mindset. While the person who is successful may have hated their job, they decided to embrace it as an opportunity to grow. The other person may have only seen it as a hindrance. It's possible for you to find pleasure in unpleasant situations. You just have to shift your focus.

Mindset is one of the biggest driving forces to success. On the other hand a negative mindset can be a great hindrance. Our mindset plays a major part in the quality of life that we will experience. In fact, Steve Maraboli, author of *Life, Truth, and Being Free* said, "Once your mindset changes, everything on the outside will change with it." To some, this may be no great mystery. Most people know that attitude determines altitude. However, what one may be lacking is the constant reminder that we must take control of our mind in order to take control of our lives.

The battlefield is within; the battlefield is in the mind. Each day, we are fed thoughts, ideas, notions and doubts that penetrate our psyche and play a vital role in our daily actions and pursuits. While I don't subscribe to the notion that someone can cause you to be unsuccessful or disadvantaged, I am fully aware of the reality that what you hear, see and perceive plays a part in what you do, feel and believe. You may have suffered psychological, mental and emotional abuse, which may have affected your quality of life greatly. However, instead of staying wounded and scarred, regain control of your mind, fight against the negativity, and feed your mind with fresh new ideas and thoughts.

This is why Paul urged in Romans 12:2, *"Be transformed by the renewing of your mind."* Until your mind is transformed and renewed, you will continue on the downward spiraling pattern of blame, discontentment and unachieved goals. You must decide that you have the keys to unlock your heart's desires. In order to become great, you must take responsibility for your life and actions. Never forget—it all begins with you.

FINAL THOUGHT

There is an immense price for greatness—that price is responsibility. You must be responsible for your greatness by being accountable for your actions and deeds. Be sure that you constantly remind yourself that greatness begins and ends with you. You are the single most important piece in this puzzle called greatness. No matter how gifted, talented or connected you may be, the onus is on you to unleash the greatness that's within.

3

THE POWER OF FAITH
OVERCOMING DOUBT

Faith is a knowledge within the heart, beyond the reach of proof.
– Khalil Gibran

If you look at the societal greats, you will notice that at the core of their success is a belief system upon which they stand. Anyone who is or hopes to become successful must have faith. Faith causes you to see the unseen, move the unmovable, and reach the unreachable. Furthermore, faith causes you to believe and work toward what some might consider impossible. *Faith is the substance of things hoped for, the evidence of things not seen* (Hebrews 11:1). Faith adds substance to what you are hoping for, and assures you that what you are believing for is possible.

Although something may not be physically present, faith

believes that it's there. Therefore, whatever you desire, believe that it will happen. Declare to yourself that it has to happen. If you can believe it, you can achieve it. Les Brown put it this way, "It's not only possible to live your dreams; it's necessary." Faith serves as the bridge for you to take your dreams from thought to reality. Faith is literally the link that connects you to the realization of your dreams and goals.

There is no denying the power of faith. In order to be successful in any endeavor, it is imperative that you possess faith. Your faith doesn't have to be magnanimous. You just have to simply believe. You have to reach deep down inside and realize that you are full of potential and greatness. Anything is possible if you believe. Jesus said, *If you can believe, all things are possible*...(Mark 9:23 NKJV).

Furthermore, faith causes you to attempt and accomplish things that many may view as impossible. Faith is that driving force that pushes you past all doubts, fears and obstacles to accomplish your goals. Without faith, you will never have the life that you desire. Without faith, you can never be who God intended you to be. Without faith, it is impossible to obtain success, it's impossible to realize your dreams, and it's impossible to please God.

Faith aligns everything for you. With faith, your dreams, your abilities, and God's power come together to help you achieve great success. Faith opens doors. It simply makes things happen. Regardless of how difficult things might get in your life, faith keeps you on course. It is the foundation that you can stand on in a rocky world. It is like a tank that shields you during the time of war. Faith will ultimately be the platform on which you stand to receive the reward of greatness that you have worked so hard to achieve.

Believe

Norman Vincent Peale said, "Believe in yourself! Have faith in your abilities! Without a humble but reasonable

> *Faith will ultimately be the platform on which you stand to receive the reward of greatness that you have worked so hard to achieve.*

confidence in your own powers, you cannot be successful or happy." It is necessary to have confidence and faith in your own greatness. Have confidence that the gifts you hold have the power to cause you to become great. Believe in yourself and believe in God. Tremendous accomplishments are in store for you.

Many people say, "What you see is what you get." This saying is often in response to a person that has demanded something greater or different from what they see. Oddly enough, life is this way. Situations arise and the response is, "What you see is what you get." Sadly, many people consent to whatever life throws at them.

Life will sometimes show you poverty, lack of opportunity and growth, and moral decay. If we are not careful, we will accept this as the norm. But I challenge you to *believe*. I challenge you to believe for bigger and better. I dare you to look life in the face and demand more from it than you have experienced in the past.

One day while I was at work, I thought, *there has to be more to life than this.* My job appeared to be a dead end and I could feel the ceiling closing in on me. Reminiscing on that day, I remember being frustrated. I thought about the dreams I had of becoming wealthy and prosperous. I looked at my present situation and almost got sucked into the thought that perhaps my life would never change. But suddenly, I gained a fresh perspective and got the revelation that my life can and will get better. In that moment, I chose to believe that something greater was in store for me.

With that thought in mind, I made the necessary steps to achieve the life that God had destined for me to live. First, I looked at my current work situation. Despite what I had initially considered to be limits and boundaries, I worked even harder. Something good had to come as a result of my efforts. I told myself that if I worked hard, my efforts couldn't be overlooked. I was eventually promoted twice in the next few months. In addition, I won the districts *"Above and Beyond – Employee of the Year Award."*

After my professional advancement, I assessed other areas of my life. I decided that I would pursue my dream of being a professional speaker. I recognized that I had a desire to speak, and my love for helping people gave me the fuel to start. However, I was still hesitant. I was doubtful. Like many, I allowed what people thought, my past, my lack of experience and lack of education to hinder my efforts. But in those moments of doubt, it is important to have faith. Despite what people think, despite what you may not have, when God calls you to something, you have to believe what He put in you is more than enough to complete the task at hand.

Despite what comes against you to hinder or stop you, use your faith as the driving force to roll over those obstacles. God reminded me that He gave me the dream and that He has enabled and gifted me to carry out that dream. I soon emerged from the ashes of doubt and despair, and *D.R. Speaks* was born.

Having to cross over into different arenas and styles of speaking was new and even uncomfortable at times. I had my reservations initially. But what God had called me to was bigger than any doubter. It was in fact bigger than me. I started hosting a weekly radio broadcast called, "I've Got Something to Say" and a few short weeks later, I started my business, *D.R. Speaks Enterprises, LLC.* Never in a hundred years would I have thought that I would become an entrepreneur, but I stepped out on faith. After multiple speaking engagements, workshops and events, not only have I made my dreams come true, but I have positioned myself by faith to continue on the road to success and greatness.

Take the First Step

Dr. Martin Luther King, Jr. said, "You may not be able to see the whole staircase, but take the first step." The unfortunate reality in life is that many of us never get started because of what we see at the bottom of the staircase. Society has taught us that seeing is believing. However, I beg to differ, because we are to *"walk by faith, not by sight."* Faith allows you to climb those steps even when you don't know where the staircase may take you. *Believing is seeing.* Your faith will provide the necessary vision to take the steps toward greatness.

Most times, it's simply about taking the first step. Often, the road is revealed to us as we travel. Our vision and focus becomes clearer as we take more steps. Certain things will only be revealed to us through the process of pursuing our goals.

For example, Steve Jobs, along with a group of friends, started Apple with a sole focus on computers. However, over the years, Apple has become infamous for its innovations in the cellular phone industry with the iPhone. Apple not only introduced the iPhone, but also broke into the music industry with the iPod and iTunes. Had Jobs never got started, he would have never realized the opportunities that were available to him. Furthermore, most of what we know Apple to be today was later revealed to them in the pursuit of other goals.

My advice to you is to simply get started. Launch out into the deep. Yes it may be frightful and the way may be unclear. But as you walk, know that each step is ordered by God. In due time, He will reveal the necessary things to you in order to become and stay successful.

Overcoming the Biggest Enemy

If I asked you who your biggest enemy is, you might say the devil. You might say the government or even someone who has always seemingly had it out for you. However, if you've been paying attention thus far, you should know by now that I don't subscribe to these theories. The biggest enemy that you and I will ever face is self. We are our own worst enemies. Often, we are the first to psyche ourselves out, and quite honestly, it's sad. I can't count the number of individuals that I have encountered professionally, socially and personally who have no faith in their own abilities and talents.

People constantly make excuses as to why they can't move forward in their dreams. If they don't have enough money to get started, they think no one will support them. Others are hesitant because there are many other people doing what they themselves believe they are called to do. Perhaps, they don't believe that they are connected to the right people, or they doubt that they have the right resources.

These thoughts don't exist unless you place them there. I'm

not saying don't consider start-up costs and competitive advantage. But don't count yourself out when you haven't even put forth any real effort. By all means count up the cost. But focus more on the gain, and less on what you might lose. There are endless possibilities available for those who are willing to overcome doubt by maintaining their faith.

Move yourself and the doubts that you have out of the way in order to see the possibilities of your dreams. Look at yourself the way God sees you. Believe in the gifts, talents and skills that He has placed within you. No matter what those gifts may be, know that they are powerful and great. They will ultimately assist you in reaching your full potential.

The option is yours. You can believe what God says or you can believe what others think. Limited thinking will only take you so far. Tap into the vision that God has given you. Embrace who it is that He created you to be and realize that all

Believe in God and believe in yourself.

things are possible to them that believe. Have faith and doubt not. Believe in God and believe in yourself. You will get better, and you will ultimately achieve what you may have once thought was impossible.

When you move yourself out of the way, and replace your doubts with belief and faith in God, nothing and no one will be able to stop you. Regardless of what storms may arise in your life, keep the faith. Remember, *faith is the substance of things hoped for, and the evidence of things not seen.* In other words, faith is being sure that what you believe will manifest itself in your life, despite its present absence. When you maintain your faith in God, yourself and your abilities, you will access the true power faith. Thus enabling you to consistently overcome doubt.

FINAL THOUGHT

The things that you hope to accomplish in life require faith. You can't survive without faith. Yes, it may be hard to believe at times, but it's necessary that you hold fast to your faith. Faith will allow you to understand that you are yet becoming who you were created and destined to be. Furthermore, your faith has the ability to make impossible situations possible. When you understand this, you can keep the faith and continue striving toward your goals and dreams. It will all be worth it in the end.

4

THE POWER OF ACTION
MAKE A DECISION

"If you want to make a difference, you have to make a decision."
– Eric Thomas

If you are anything like me, I am sure that you can always find areas in your life that need improvement. However, I recognize that it takes more than just a desire to change. It takes action. In order to have your desires fulfilled, there must be action that corresponds to those desires.

So many people are not satisfied with their current situations. Many are frustrated with their financial situations and there are countless individuals who aren't content with their professional, educational or ministerial accomplishments. There are some who are just simply unhappy. But even with all of the issues that we face, I recognize that we all have the ability to choose what type of life we live.

We have all been given the ability to make decisions regarding our lives, and we choose what actions we will take. Our lives are the sum of our decision making processes, or lack thereof. The decisions that we make help shape and mold our lives into what we desire. There is a plan and purpose designed for each of our lives that will require an earnest diligence. When you consider all that you have been blessed with, you must realize that we have a responsibility to be faithful stewards over all that God has placed in our hands.

Be Faithful Over Little

In order to have lives of fulfillment and abundance, we must be committed to the work assigned to us. In *The Butler,* a movie by Lee Daniels, it was interesting to note how diligent the butler was. He went from being a local restaurant waiter to being a butler in the White House, where he served numerous presidents. Due to his faithfulness as a waiter, and his willingness to be faithful over the little that he had, he achieved great success.

The first time I heard motivational speaker, teacher and author, Eric Thomas, in person was at Eastern Michigan University. What I remember most from his message was the profound way in which he conveyed the biblical principle found in

Matthew 25:23, which explains that if you are faithful over little, God will make you ruler over much. He made it clear that it wasn't his ability to speak that got him where he is today. It was his

> *In order to have lives of fulfillment and abundance, we must be committed to the work assigned to us..*

faithfulness and commitment to the little things that seemingly had nothing to do with his dreams. Sometimes, we are placed in situations that, at first glance, have absolutely nothing to do with our dreams. However, you will discover that these experiences are necessary.

In the original *Karate Kid*, when the young Daniel Larusso was initially being trained by Mr. Miyagi, he had him washing and waxing cars. Daniel thought the exercises were useless, but later found out that the motions and discipline that he exhibited by washing and waxing cars would pay off in battle. You will encounter battles in life that will require the use of some skill or resource acquired that you may have initially thought to be useless. Therefore, despise not small beginnings. Never shun and discount certain experiences as useless. Everything that we experience helps instruct us in our decision-making processes.

Get to Work

I'm sure there are times in life when you wish you weren't so idle. You wish you would have acted at the time, but you did nothing. There is no worse feeling than knowing that you decided to stand still in a situation when you should have acted.

My biggest moment of regret came the night my mother died. I was only nine years old when she passed. But even as I grew older, I always believed I could have done something to prevent her passing. However, the reality is, I will never know. I just simply have to deal with the decision that I made to do nothing, and live with it. You see, sometimes, not making a decision at all can be as detrimental as making bad decisions.

You can't afford to sit idly by, expecting for situations to simply work themselves out. Don't be afraid to get dirty. Don't be afraid to be hurt or disappointed. It is better to have tried something and failed than to have not tried at all, wondering what could have been.

So many of us desire change and we want better, yet we do absolutely nothing to change our circumstances. Remember, *it all begins with you*. You have to recognize that you, and you alone, are responsible for the actions and inactivity in your life. In chapter three, I told you to believe because fear and unbelief stifles us and causes us to become stagnant.

If we are going to make a difference, we are going to have to make decisions that will produce the change we want to see. We have to be willing to work and put forth the necessary actions to become better. Once you decide to act, things will line up with what it is that you have set out to accomplish. Tony Robbins said, "It is in your moments of decision that your destiny is shaped."

Your decision making ultimately helps shape your life and destiny. Whatever you want to happen in your

Making the right decisions today will help alleviate a lot of heartache later.

life, you have to make a decision to make it happen. If you want that promotion, go for it. If you want to grow your business, put in the work to make it happen. Whatever your dreams or goals are, realize that you are the only one standing between you and your dreams coming true.

Making Wise Decisions

If we are ever going to be great, we have to be sure that not only must we *make a decision*, but we must be sure that we are making *wise* decisions. On the path to greatness, be sure that the decisions you make will be beneficial to you in the long run. Being idle and not making a decision can bring about immense regret. Furthermore, making foolish decisions can be even more detrimental.

Making the right decisions today will help alleviate a lot of heartache later. The decisions you make today will shape the life that you will live tomorrow. If you make bad decisions, you will have to deal with the lasting effects of negative repercussions. However, if you commit to doing what is right, good things will follow you. Proverbs 11:19 (ESV) says, *"Always do the right thing, and you will live."* In the world that we live in, this can be very difficult at times.

Making wise decisions is all about awareness. You have to be aware of the repercussions of foolish decisions, as well as the rewards of positive decisions. Furthermore, one must be aware of their ability to make the right choices. Many people believe they have no other choice but to live lives of moral ruin. They consent to the fast life of crime, perversion and sin, as if they have no other options. Their awareness of a better life is marred by what they see around them.

Perhaps, this is you. Maybe you find yourself in a dead-end situation in your current profession. Maybe you are struggling in your educational pursuits. Your perception could very well be marred, and your awareness of bigger and better things might be restricted. Opportunities for advancement, betterment and growth are all around you. Despite what society defines as the norm, remember that there is greatness within you.

Therefore, you don't have to settle for mediocrity. Demand the best. To that end, be sure that you seek opportunity. Seek the life that you want. If, for some reason, you can't find what you are looking for, create it. Whatever you do, don't forgo wise decision making. Your decision making is paramount to the success that you desire.

But It's Worth It

I would be remiss if I let you believe that simply doing right is going to make everything perfect in your life. Just because you make the right decisions doesn't always mean that things will work in your favor. In fact, you may do what you know to be correct, but may still face ridicule, loss or pain as a result. However, realize that doing what is right will always pay off in the long run. Therefore, even if making the right choice doesn't quite work out as you planned, you can have peace in knowing that you made the right decision.

Consider those in history who stood up against injustice. Nelson Mandela, for example, was ultimately imprisoned for doing what he believed was right. Because of his beliefs, he was sentenced to nearly thirty years in prison. Mandela was not wrong for what he believed. In fact, he was right the whole time.

It was many years later that the world, and the nation of South Africa, finally realized that Nelson Mandela was right all along, and that he should no longer be punished for his actions. When you look at people like Martin Luther King, Jr., Rosa Parks, Mahatma Gandhi and even Jesus Christ, all of these individuals faced unwanted pressure and consequences by opposing forces because of what they believed.

Martin Luther King, Jr. knew that segregation, racism and prejudices weren't right; therefore, he stood against it. His fight against injustice ultimately cost him his life. Rosa Parks decided to withstand inequality by staying seated on the bus in a seat that was reserved for non-colored passengers. Parks was ultimately arrested and suffered much ridicule as a result of her decision.

Gandhi was also imprisoned for his role as a civil rights activist. Despite knowing what the consequences may have been, he still held firm to his conviction. Gandhi exhibited a quiet strength that shows you must be willing to stand up for what is right, despite the consequences that may ensue.

Jesus Christ, who was sinless, was crucified for simply being Himself and carrying out the assignment that He came to earth to fulfill. There were many who did not understand, nor did they agree with Jesus' teachings, actions or deeds. They considered Him to be a violator of their law when, in fact, all He desired was for mankind to be free—as God intended for us to be.

Despite what all of the aforementioned persons suffered, they were all vindicated and got the victory in the end. Yes, Martin Luther King, Jr. may have lost his life for fighting for civil rights, but Heaven was his reward. Furthermore, he, along with Gandhi and Parks, would eventually win the hearts of the people. These icons are still celebrated today as heroes in civil rights. Thousands of years later, there are billions of people who subscribe to the teachings of Christianity. They believe that although Jesus was crucified, He rose three days later and is in Heaven now seated at the right hand of the Father.

Understand that there will always be opposition when you set out to do well. Where good is present, evil is somewhere nearby, waiting to stick its head up to deter you from making wise decisions. Regardless of what consequences you may face, you have to be willing to endure the hardship and stand for what you know to be right.

Don't allow the pressures of peers and society to cause you to act out of character. Don't allow the words of the naysayers to persuade you to another thought and way of doing things. Romans 12:21 (ESV) says, *Do not be not overcome by evil, but overcome evil with good.* Our greatest weapon against evil is to combat it with good. When you do good, you will receive good. It may not always be immediate, and in many cases, it may not come in the way that you expect it, *but it's worth it.* Don't lose sight of the reward for doing the right thing. Don't be weary in doing well, because in due season you will reap if you don't give up.

The severity of our decision making is enormous. Becoming a better employee, a better spouse or a better friend hinges upon your ability to make the decisions necessary to warrant the growth that you seek. At the end of the day, remember that you have been given the ability to choose. Just be sure that you choose your actions wisely. Your future depends on it. *If you want to make a difference, you have to make a decision.*

FINAL THOUGHT

Don't be afraid to put forth the necessary action in order to have the life that you desire. If you want something, go after it. The world is full of opportunities for those willing to seize them. Nothing happens if you remain idle. You have to act in order to make things happen. Make wise, calculated, and purpose-driven decisions. If you do so, greatness is sure to be the end result.

5

THE POWER OF VISION
I CAN SEE CLEARLY NOW

"In order to carry a positive action, we must develop here a positive vision."–Dalai Lama

As we are on the journey toward greatness, we must first be able to discern how we are going to get there. Vision gives that direction. Vision allows you to see the goal and the dream that you have becoming a reality. Vision says, "It's going to happen." Vision says, "It has to happen." Vision shows you how something is going to happen, why something is going to happen, where something is going to happen, and even when it is going to happen. That's vision.

Vision is so essential in unleashing the greatness within that, without a vision, we will perish. People without vision have no meaning to their existence; hence they live flaccid, unfilled lives.

They have no true joy, peace or contentment. Lack of vision kills dreams. It kills pursuits, desires, and it ultimately kills the spirit of a person. Without vision, there is no clear understanding, no clear road, and no clear trail to follow in order to reach your goal and realize your dreams. You *must* have vision.

Vision is given to individuals to guide them in the pursuit of their dreams and goals. That's why my prayer is always, "God, give me vision." With vision you gain precision, clarity and focus. It helps one to perceive things in a better light. When you tap into vision, you will truly understand that vision is so much more than just the ability to see something with the human eye.

The great thing about vision is that it gives you a clear understanding of what it is you are able to accomplish. However, *Vision shows you how something is going to happen, why something is going to happen, where something is going to happen, and even when it is going to happen.* many people have a vision, but allow distractions to stop them from carrying out that vision. They let doubt creep in and they begin to question themselves: "Am I ready? Can I do this?" These are what Antoine Jackson, author of *100 Watt Life,* calls, "self-limiting thoughts." Instead of allowing these thoughts to blur your vision, remain determined that you are going to stay focused on what you set out to do. What you see for your life is possible, and the greatness within you will help bring the vision to pass.

HAVE A PICTURE OF SUCCESS IN YOUR MIND

What does the vision that you have for yourself look like? Do you even know? How can you realize something has arrived if you are unsure of what it looks like? You must clarify what you want out of your life in order to ascertain what you desire.

For too long, I pursued things that were a complete waste of time because I had no clear vision of success. I knew I wanted to be successful. I knew I wanted to be wealthy. However, I did not know what it looked like. The thing that you desire has to be so clear that you can almost reach out and touch it. It has to be so real that you can taste it. Get a picture of what you want in your mind, and don't quit until that picture becomes reality.

Consider the picture frames on the wall in the store that have no pictures inside. I've always wondered why some stores didn't put pictures inside those frames. If the stores would put a picture inside that frame, at least the potential buyer could see the true potential of the frame.

A frame is only as good as the picture that goes in it. Success may be what you want; however, without a picture of that success, all you have is a frame. There are certain frames required for certain pictures. Without a clear picture, you will never know what type of frame is required to hold that picture.

Regardless of what you want in life, your *picture* (vision) is important. Knowing what the picture looks like will determine what type frame of you need to compliment your picture. In other words, your vision for success will help determine the necessary steps to reach that success. If your dream is to become a doctor, there are steps that you must take. Perhaps you want to graduate college, start a business or build a successful ministry. There are steps that you must take in order to make these things happen. Identify your vision—your picture of success and greatness. Then you will be able to apply the correct frame—the necessary actions.

Stay Focused

Reflect on the goals that you have for your life. Maybe in the beginning of a new year, after a birthday, or after a major life event, you set goals for your life. Have you accomplished any of them? Have you identified the necessary steps in order to better yourself? Are you doing what is required in order for you to experience the success that you yearn for? If not, why aren't you on that road to success?

I've made these inquiries simply to cause you to reflect. I've posed these questions to get your mind back focused on the things that *you* said you were going to do. In order for dreams to come true, it is essential that you have vision.

Many of you have said that you would start a business, write a book, or even go back to school. Some of you have said that you would work harder to get the promotion that you desire, or to grow your current business. For some reason, in your attempt to check these things off of your list, you got deterred and are no longer in pursuit of your dreams and goals.

However, there are also some of you that don't quite fit into this category. You are excelling and have been crossing things off your to-do list expediently. For that, I commend you. If you are in that number, stay on track and continue to reach toward your goals. Regardless of what position you currently find yourself in, vision is the one tool that will help you navigate through the process of becoming great.

Often in our daily pursuit of our goals and dreams, we are challenged and forced to reconsider if our dreams are viable. Focus less on what you *see* and more on what you believe. Second Corinthians 5:7 says, *"Walk by faith, not by sight."* Allow your faith to guide you past the challenges that you will face. Your faith will assist your vision and empower you to see beyond your present perils. This is true vision.

Bishop J. Drew Sheard said, "You must see it before you see it, or you will never see it." In other words, you must have a vision for what you want before it becomes a reality, or it will never happen. Furthermore, you must have faith in what you believing for. Don't allow the negativity that you witness daily, or the lack of achieved goals, to cause your vision to become distorted. As long as you are working toward your goal, and you remain focused, you will eventually possess what you envisioned.

VISION IS CUSTOMIZED SIGHT

I am fond of optical analogies. In my time as a certified optician, I have learned that vision and sight are two completely different things. There is a thin line between the two, but they are stark contrasts of each other. Sight can be blurry, dim, spotty or cloudy. In fact, a person can be considered legally blind, but still have the ability to see to a certain degree. A person who is having visual discomfort and struggling with sight lacks vision. Vision is clarity, focus, precision and acuity. Therefore, in order to receive vision, the visual disparities that a person is experiencing must be corrected. In order for this

> *Vision is tailor-made sight, customized to help maximize your visual spectrum.*

to happen, visual assistance must be prescribed. This is why people wear glasses, contacts and even have corrective eye procedures. But what is prescribed to improve one person's vision may not work for another. Vision is tailor-made sight, customized to help you maximize *your* visual spectrum.

My glasses are useless for someone who has a greater or lesser need for vision correction. If their prescribed vision enhancers require a higher number of diopters (power) than mine, they would only grow frustrated wearing my glasses. Life is the same way. Oftentimes, we are so preoccupied with what someone is doing or what someone else has obtained that it causes us to lose focus of our goals. We have to realize they are operating with a vision that is tailor-made for them. You have to wear the vision that is designed for you. When you live life with your prescribed vision, it will greatly reduce the stress and worry that comes with trying to live life through someone else's vision.

PROTECT THE VISION

People will often doubt your goals and dreams because they can't *see* how you're going to achieve them. However, in these times remind yourself that it's not their vision. Understand that those people who aren't connected to you won't be able see the vision clearly. It has been prescribed for you.

> *If you are going to see your vision come to pass, you are going to have to protect it.*

It is important for you to recognize that your vision is custom-made. If you are going to see your vision come to pass, you are going to have to protect it.

For those of you who have been very successful, and are living the lives that you hoped to live, keep up the good work. In essence, you may not need vision assistance. You may in fact have 20/20 vision. If this is the case, allow me to give you a few tips to help you maintain success. For those of you taking the steps toward unleashing your greatness, here is what you need to do going forward:

1. *Be aware of your surroundings:* During my tenure as an optician, I've seen people who once had perfect vision, but at some point suffered an eye injury that handicapped them in their eyesight. You could sustain an injury to your eye while on the job, playing sports, and many other activities. Injuries sustained to the eye can cause you to become permanently blind. Being aware of your surroundings can help prevent possible injuries to your sight. In other words, be aware of people and experiences that can damage your vision. You must be alert, and be sure that you place yourself in situations that will be beneficial to your success and betterment. You can't afford to damage your vision due to carelessness.

2. *Wear the proper eyewear:* In the aforementioned paragraph, I mention how people sustain eye injuries on the job. Often, this is because a person failed to wear protective eyewear that would have otherwise prevented their injury. Furthermore, there is another form of eyewear that everyone should wear, and that is sunglasses. Sunglasses give your eyes the protection needed to shield your eyes from harmful UV rays, which can compromise the integrity of your eye health and greatly affect your vision.

   Oddly enough, most of us revere the sun as a good thing. The sun provides an invaluable resource in helping us live healthy lives. However, there is the adage that says, *too much of a good thing can actually be a bad thing*. Excessive exposure to the sun can cause many health problems. Furthermore, continual sun exposure to the eye can cause premature cataracts, which can eventually cause blindness. Therefore, sunglasses are an invaluable asset to vision protection.

We have to be sure that we take the supposed good things in moderation. The point is to protect yourself from things that can harm your vision. Avoid things that appear to be good for you, but can actually turn out to be detrimental to your success. It's alright to have fun. It's okay to be in relationships and enjoy life in general. But like the sun, too much of a good thing can cause issues in the long run. Therefore, funnel all of life's enjoyment through the accomplishment of your goals. Don't allow things and people to block your vision and blind you from your goals. You must be intentional and calculated in what you do. Consider how your actions will affect every area of your life. Some things may be good, but be aware of the effect they can have on your life.

3. *Maintain a healthy diet:* It is necessary that you maintain good physical health in order to maintain good vision. A healthy diet is a vital asset. Like sustaining good visual acuity requires a good diet, so it is in your life when it comes to maintaining a vision for your life. Feed yourself with things that aid in bringing the vision to fruition. If you want to be a successful speaker, study other great speakers. If you want to become the

next manager, director or president at your current place of employment, feed yourself with things that will get you closer to that vision.

Be sure that you don't feed yourself with junk that will hinder and diminish the quality of your vision. Don't allow negativity, nor the taste of harmful things, to cause you to miss out on the best of your vision. Ultimately, a bad diet will hinder the strength of your vision and cause it to diminish much quicker than it may have ordinarily.

WRITE THE VISION

In the Bible, in the book of Habakkuk, God instructed the prophet to write the vision and make

> *...the vision God gives you isn't for you alone. It's also for those who are connected to you.*

it plain. This allowed the people to see it and carry out the work that God charged them to complete. Recognize that the vision God gives you isn't for you alone. It's also for those who are connected to you. You must write the vision and make it plain. Make it clear so that you can take the necessary steps to bring the vision to reality.

In business, a common belief is that the vision is not real until you have laid it out before you. It is encouraged that you keep a record of what you desire. Draw it out on a vision board or collaborate with others who can help bring your vision to pass. The vision that you have is useless as long as it is hidden. People will often ignore or overlook what you say unless they can see something tangible that is in line with what you said.

I recall when I got engaged. Porsha and I were very excited. We both were nervous, and we really didn't know what to expect. Of course, the first thing we did was tell our family and friends. Then one Sunday, right before I preached a sermon, I made the announcement to the entire church that we were getting married. It was two years from the date I proposed that we actually tied the knot. However, the journey up until that point was interesting, to say the least.

We had a difficult time trying to determine when our actual wedding date would be. I wanted to get married sooner than later, while she was pretty adamant on finishing her last year of school. Furthermore, throughout our engagement, I ran into some financial challenges that imposed against the wedding day plans. When we saw people at various functions, they always asked us when the actual wedding would take place. At times, we thought we had a date and other times, we were still trying to decide. We probably changed our intended wedding date at least four or five times. Many doubted that a wedding would ever happen.

We did more talking than we did planning. There were long periods of time when we didn't put any action forth. We never really committed to any contractors. The dates that we settled on were never anything more than suggestions—we never wrote the vision that we had for our wedding. It wasn't until we wrote the vision and made it plain that things fell into place. We printed save-the-date cards. We finalized our bridal party and had a meeting with them. We shared the date, the venue, the time, and even the color scheme with the entire team. We made the vision plain to them.

Once we conveyed our wedding plans to others, the excitement and the buzz stirred. People joined us in our efforts to bring the vision to pass. The vision was clear to them now as well, and they wanted to play their part in helping make it a reality. Two years from the date that I proposed, on January 28, 2012, we had the wedding that we both envisioned. The vision did come to pass.

In order for your dreams and visions to become a reality, you must construct what it looks like. Move the vision from your head to something tangible. Habakkuk had a great vision and received very precise instructions from God. However, what God gave him had to be presented to those who were expected to help Habakkuk accomplish the vision. The people were able to run with the vision because it was presented to them in a plain, tangible way.

It is essential that you lay out the vision for what you desire. Then and only then will the steps necessary be made plain for you to see. Write the vision and make it plain.

FINAL THOUGHT

The vision that you have for your life, business, ministry or career will ultimately serve as a blueprint for how you will accomplish your goals. Where there is no vision, the people perish (Proverbs 29:18 KJV). This would suggest that without a vision, I have no clear understanding or plan as to how I am going to fulfill my desires. Without such a plan, my dream will die, my plans will go unfulfilled, and thus my life will be a dead end. I must have vision if I am to ever discover and unleash the greatness within.

6

THE POWER OF POTENTIAL
YOU HAVE WHAT IT TAKES

"Never underestimate the power of dreams and the influence of the human spirit. We are all the same in this notion: The potential for greatness lives within each of us." – Wilma Rudolph

The potential to be great is truly within us all. We all have a purpose, and we have the potential to fulfill it. The skills, talents and gifts that we have can all be used to impact the world. Furthermore, the time that we have been given on this earth is precious. Therefore, it is imperative that we make the most of the time that we have. When time runs out, our life runs out and our ability to make a difference is null and void. Use your time wisely. Live your life with purpose, and decide that you will make the most out of the life that you have been blessed with.

Get Your Priorities in Order

As you evaluate your life, goals and dreams, prioritize things in order of least important to most important. Make sure that vital areas of importance aren't neglected. In a world full of people who seem to have their priorities confused, it is imperative that you focus on the important issues in your life. In order to move your life from potential to purpose, you have to maintain your priorities.

While I was in college at Michigan State University, many people had designer clothing and shoes, the latest phones, and they always found a way to be at all the major social events. Yet, many of these people had these things at the expense of their books, food or even tuition being paid. While there is nothing wrong with having nice things, there is major detriment that is bound to ensue when these things take priority over things that can actually add value to your life.

Assess how your actions benefit your life and contribute to those around you. If you can't find any value in the decisions that you make, consider switching things up a bit. Like Antoine Jackson says, "Flip the switch. Change the bulb. Whatever you do, decide to shine." In other words, do what must be done in order to shine and make a difference. Don't allow your purpose to be diminished by poor prioritization.

We all have purpose. One major purpose that we all have is to help others live the lives that they desire as well. What are you doing today that will benefit someone else tomorrow? Are you making a difference with your life? If you can't answer this question positively, reassess your priorities and strive to keep the main thing the main thing.

Don't Cast Your Pearls Among Swine

The Bible recounts one of the teachings of Jesus, which said, *Don't cast your pearls among swine for fear that they*

> *Focus less on those who don't appreciate you, and focus more on how you can make an impact in the lives of those that will.*

trample them under their feet (Matthew 7:6). Here Jesus tries to convey that pigs merely don't have the ability to appreciate what you may consider valuable. The same goes with some people and pursuits in our lives. There are some desires that we have that simply aren't worth our time and effort. Furthermore, there are some people who simply won't appreciate what you have to offer.

Therefore, when it comes to your gift, value it. Don't allow people to diminish, belittle or devalue your gift. Don't allow people to cause you to lose sight of what you have to offer. Focus less on those who don't appreciate you, and focus more on how you can make an impact in the lives of those that will. If you take nothing else from this subject, please remember that opportunities will present themselves for you to compromise your greatness, but you must never concede.

One major pitfall is using your gifts, skills and resources for the wrong purpose. It's sad to have the ability to do so many great things, yet choose to focus these things in the wrong areas. Place value on your life and gifts. You are special. Your life is special and it is meant to be valued and appreciated.

There will be pigs that will bait you into casting your pearls among them. People will attempt to sell your life short with cheap, aimless and unfulfilled opportunities. Don't waste your life. As my friend Kellen Brooks says, "You only have one life to live, don't throw it away."

WHAT'S IN YOUR HANDS?

We've learned thus far, the importance of recognizing and releasing the greatness within by sharing our gifts with the world. Also, we have learned that we all have the potential to be great. However, oftentimes, we doubt that we have the skills and talents necessary to even make a difference. Sometimes, we are called to perform certain tasks, whether it is at work, school or even church. We become preoccupied with the thought that perhaps we aren't fit for the task. I've been there many times before. When God called me to the ministry to preach His word, my initial thought was, *Lord, are you sure?* I doubted that I had the ability to do what God asked me to do.

You may be faced with similar issues. You may be one who is constantly prodded by others to take action in a certain area. Have you ever been encouraged to pursue a business, career or a dream because someone recognized greatness within you that you had yet to realize? How often have you been told that you should pursue a certain goal? Some people even remind you of your greatness daily. However, you might have psyched yourself out and came up with various excuses as to why you can't get the job done.

We might have some reservations about our abilities and we may not have the faith to take the first step. But we must realize that we are often our own worst enemies. When we view ourselves in a negative light, it is often an unfair and inaccurate observation. It is real easy to look at yourself and count the reasons why you can't succeed, be great, or pursue your dreams. It wouldn't take much effort at all to list all of the things that you lack. However, I want you to focus less on what you *don't* have, and focus more on what you *do* have. Whether you believe it or not, what you have is the very thing that will push you into your purpose.

Moses was responsible for delivering the Israelites, who were in Egyptian bondage. When Moses was called by God, he made excuse after excuse as to why he could not complete the task. Moses did not believe that he was the one for the job. He listed all of his handicaps and misfortunes instead of focusing on the good. He looked at his speech problem. He then tried to reason with God by saying that the people wouldn't receive him, and that Pharaoh would never let the people go. In addition, Moses recognized that he didn't have a great army, and that going head up against Pharaoh could cost his life. Even though Moses had very legitimate concerns, God asked Moses to focus on what was in his hand.

God, instead of pacifying the fears of Moses, challenged him to take a look at things from a different perspective. God simply asked Moses, *"What is that in your hands?"* (Exodus 4:2 NLT). When God asked Moses what was in his hand, it was to enlighten him to the fact that he had something to work with, something that could help him be successful in his pursuits. He simply wanted Moses to focus on what he had instead of what Moses believed he was lacking.

All that Moses seemingly had was a stick. Moses did not recognize the power in what he possessed. God showed Moses that it was much more than a stick; it was more than what met Moses' eye. Like Moses, you possess something that is powerful beyond what you can conceive. If you look at things the way God views them, you will see that what's in your hands is very powerful. You will see that greatness is right at your fingertips.

Work With What You Have

Make the best of every situation. Make the best of your gifts, talents, resources and opportunities. Some things might seem minor, but how you handle them could yield great results. No matter where you may find yourself at this point in your life—educated or not, rich or poor—what you have is enough to make a difference. If you needed more, you would have more.

I am partial to the scripture that says, *God will supply all your needs according to His riches in glory* (Phil. 4:19 ESV). You already possess whatever you need to fulfill your assignment on earth. Those gifts that God has placed within you are what is going to be used to fulfill that assignment. Again, it may seem minor to you now. However, the little that you have now is going to produce greater. Sadly, many people despise what they have now and never pursue anything greater.

Despise not small beginnings because everything that we know to be great was once considered small. What would happen to a farmer if he shunned the seed, which he needs to bring forth the harvest, because of the size of the seed? If he operated with that type of mentality, he would never reap the desired harvest. What if Steve Jobs had made excuses for why he couldn't make his dreams come true? Imagine if Google would have given up because they didn't have all the things in place that they wanted. Where would Amazon be right now if they despised their small beginnings? These companies all started in garages. None of these companies resembled in the beginning what they are today. But they didn't allow what they didn't have to hinder them from pursuing what they wanted.

You have to make your desires greater than your detriment. You may be in lack today, but with much effort and working with what you have, you are sure to experience wealth and great success. Make this your confession: *I have enough to make it. I have enough to get started.* Once you get started, you will see more things added to you, and more opportunities will present themselves.

For me, it all started with radio. I didn't have major sponsors or a lot of money, but I had something to say

You already possess whatever you need to fulfill your assignment on earth.

and I wanted people to hear it. I took a leap of faith, and here I stand today with a successful weekly radio program. I had to start, though.

As a result of the success of the radio show, I have more opportunities to speak and consult. I've made greater connections in business and ministry. I didn't have everything that I wanted, but I worked with what I had. I am far from where I want to be, but I'm not where I used to be. I am closer to where I desire to be than I would be had I never started.

Don't Shun What You Have

One of the biggest reasons why people never become great is because they don't fully appreciate what they have been blessed with. Oftentimes, we have a picture of what we think success and the process looks like, and we overlook what we have. In a society where we are constantly bombarded with rags to riches stories; where we see what others have that helped make them successful, we often look at ourselves and compare. More often than not, many are led to believe that they are somehow inferior to those who are successful. This is a dangerous attitude to have, and this approach will cause you to falter almost every time. Zig Ziglar said, "Success isn't measured by what you do compared to what others do. It is measured by what you do with the ability God gave you."

While it's alright to be inspired by the success of others, we must realize that we are all unique. Ultimately, this is what will make you successful. Embrace who you are and watch how that will position you into a place of power and greatness.

Don't underestimate yourself and don't count yourself out. Don't take the ignorant approach of trying to compare and compete with what everyone else is doing. Don't believe that your gift is any less powerful or special because you don't get the recognition you think it deserves. Learn to be grateful and work with what you have.

One of the most inspiring people I know is Nick Vujicic. He is an evangelist, author and speaker, but he was born without arms or legs. Instead of making excuses for what he doesn't have, and complaining about the circumstances that were handed to him, he has learned to embrace who he is. Instead of making excuses, he decided to make an impact. He now travels all over the world, inspiring people to realize that they can live life without limitations.

Refuse to accept excuses and failure. You may be like Moses and think that what you have is nothing special. But realize that freedom, peace, joy, prosperity and wealth can all be locked within that small gift, talent or purpose that you hold. Work with what you have. Don't despise or shun what you have. What's in your hands is powerful beyond measure.

FINAL THOUGHT

Think of what you possess that you can use to make an impact in the world. The impact might be small now, but start somewhere. As you use your gifts, talents and skills, you'll realize the impact is much greater than you know. Determine what you can do at home to make a difference first. Then, reach out into your community. Could your local church benefit from your gifts? Could you volunteer at a local non-profit organization? You were created for a specific purpose, and you have the potential and power to fulfill that purpose.

7

THE POWER OF A DREAM
WATCH OUT FOR DREAM KILLERS

"You intended to harm me, but God intended it all for good."

– Gen. 50:20 (NLT)

In the pursuit of greatness, achieving your goals and living your dreams, you are going to encounter "dream killers." These are people, and sometimes even circumstances, that come with one purpose and one purpose only: for you to lose sight of your dreams. Dream killers will definitely come. One just can't be sure of the time or place in which they will come. When you come in contact with dream killers, you need to be prepared. Using the biblical story of Joseph, and the experiences of others, I will outline some principles that you can use to overcome dream killers.

Don't Take It So Personal

There are certain types of people that society has characterized as haters. These are individuals who seemingly are against your success. Often these people are completely oblivious as to why you do what you do. They are often jealous because you have excelled in an area that they may desire to excel in. In short, they want what you have. Joseph's brothers were much like what society refers to as haters.

Joseph's brothers thought that he was their dad's favorite child. They thought their father esteemed Joseph above them. Furthermore, Joseph shared a dream with his brothers, in which he was in a position superior to his brothers and family. They didn't like what they heard. From there, they plotted to get rid of Joseph. None of his brothers ever asked Joseph to explain his dreams, nor did they try to understand their brother. They were simply haters. They were dream killers.

Rarely will a hater attempt to gain an understanding of your actions. They are often too consumed with envy and pride. They are incapable of treating you with fairness and celebratory esteem. When you encounter these type of people, be sure to take the high road. Don't let these people get you off track.

I encourage you to take the mentality of Joseph when dealing with these types of people: *don't take it so personal*. Joseph wasn't bitter, nor was he angry with his brothers. Joseph was so focused on his dream that nothing anyone did, or didn't do, caused him to lose his focus.

Don't allow the ignorance of others to cause you to become distracted. Hold on tight to your dreams. Fight for them and remain focused. Your dreams are too big and too valuable for you to allow dream killers to kill them. Regardless of what comes against you, keep fighting until your dreams become a reality. People may not understand you, agree with you, or support you, but that's alright. It's not their dream. It's yours. As long as you believe in you, that's all that matters.

Don't Be Concerned with the Opinions of Others

One of the toughest things to deal with when pursuing your goals and dreams are the words and opinions of others. You can't get caught up on what people

> *Don't allow the ignorance of others to cause you to become distracted. Hold on tight to your dreams.*

have to say about you. People will always have their opinions. When you consider some of the most prominent and successful people in our society, both past and present, you will notice that they all had to overcome the negative opinions of others.

- Albert Einstein was considered to be a subpar student by many of his professors. Many didn't expect him to accomplish much. However, if you browse through the archives of Einstein's accomplishments, you will find that he far surpassed the expectations and opinions of others. He single-handedly revolutionized the way we view math and science, and is considered to be one of the premier scientists in the history of mankind.

- Walt Disney was fired from the Kansas City Star for lacking imagination. He later proved that idea wrong by amassing millions of dollars by way of movie and cartoon production. Moreover, his world-acclaimed parks, Disney Land and Disney World, are visited each year by millions who are amazed at what Walt Disney's imagination produced.

- Bill Gates, founder of Microsoft, was often discouraged in his pursuit of computer technology. His family, with good intentions, encouraged Gates to pursue school over his passion for computers. Some thought he was throwing his life away once he dropped out of Harvard University. However, Gates had a dream. He believed that his dream was worth taking risks. Now years later, Microsoft is the emerging leader in the computer software industry, and Gates and his company has influenced the way we see and use technology.

Some people may have sincere intentions with their opinions. They in fact may believe that they are doing you some good by telling you what you can and cannot do. However, you have to be able to filter everything that is said through your dream. When you have a dream that is large enough, most of the noise of the naysayers, doubters and critics is drowned out by the enormity of your dream.

The Dream is Bigger than You

Pastor Daniel Grandberry is my main inspiration for this chapter. He preached a series that bears the name of this chapter. In this series, he points out how Joseph's dreams were actually God dreaming in him. Joseph's dreams were bigger than him. Although, you too have dreams, they are bigger than you. Your dream was given to you, not just to make your life better, but to better the lives of those around you. Life will get difficult, and things will occur that will make you want to give up on your dreams. But all of those who are connected to you need you to succeed.

Imagine what will happen when your dreams become a reality. Imagine the effects it will have on your family. Think about

> *Your dream was given to you, not just to make your life better, but to better the lives of those around you.*

how much your marriage and relationships will benefit. Imagine all of the lives that will be changed once you realize your dreams. No matter what you may be going through in your life right now, don't give up. People are depending on you. Your dreams are bigger than you, so don't quit.

What I like about Joseph's story is that everything that he went through was all for the benefit of himself and others. Joseph was initially sold into slavery, and then put in prison after being wrongly charged for a crime that he did not commit. Joseph spent many years as a slave and a prisoner, but eventually overcame all of that and landed at the top. Since he endured all that he went through, ending up on the winning side was a great benefit to his family, friends and countless other individuals – all because of his dream.

God is with You

Up to this point, I've mentioned everything that Joseph went through during the process of dream fulfillment. Joseph endured much pain and heartache, but scriptures reveal that God was with him through it all. As a slave, it was evident to those in authority that God was with Joseph. God's favor was so recognizable that Joseph was placed in charge of all the servants of the master's house. Unfortunately, while in the house, he was falsely accused of raping the master's wife and was thrown into prison. But even in prison, God was yet with Joseph. Even in prison, it was evident that he was special—that he was different. Joseph, despite his circumstances, still remained focused on his dreams.

It was Joseph's dream that allowed him to continue to keep the faith that one day, things would get better. Joseph was also willing to help others. While he was in prison, he met two men, a baker and a butler. Joseph used his gift to make an impression on the men, so much so that his gift was mentioned to the king and it ultimately led to his freedom. Joseph utilizing his gift was pivotal in him being freed.

It is the consistent, deliberate use of your gifts and talents that will make your dreams a reality. If you don't know what your gifts are, it will be that much harder to realize your dreams. Be sure to identify your gifts, talents and skills. They are vital in you being successful.

Throughout all of Joseph's distress, setbacks and betrayal, God was yet with him. He promises

> *It is the consistent, deliberate use of your gifts and talents that will make your dreams a reality.*

that He will never leave us, nor forsake us. When God puts a dream within you, just know that regardless of what happens in your life, your dreams will come to pass. Regardless of who stands in your way and tries to kill your dreams, remember what Paul said: *"If God is for you, who can be against you?"* (Rom. 8:31). Keep the faith, and remain focused on the end goal. Keep believing and remain locked in on your dreams so that when the dream killers come, you'll already be better, stronger and wiser.

FINAL THOUGHT

There are fewer things in life more powerful than a dreamer. A dreamer uses vision to yield limitless possibilities. Whenever life tries to seemingly hold you back and turn your life into a nightmare, remember the dream that has been given to you. Use your dream to propel you to greatness. Use your dream to encourage yourself in those rough times to help sustain your faith. Lastly, guard your dream and watch out for dream killers. They are sure to come, but when you are convinced of your dreams, nothing will be able to stop you.

8

THE POWER OF PERSEVERANCE
NEVER GIVE UP

"And let us not be weary in well doing, for in due season you will reap if you faint not." – Gal. 6:9 (ASV)

Never give up! This is the motto that I want you to rehearse when times get hard. Greatness hinges upon your ability to persevere despite the obstacles. You can't quit until you win, and even then, set another goal. You may have attempted some things that didn't work, and may constantly fall short of your dreams. Despite these setbacks, don't give up. You might have fallen down, but don't stay there. Remember the vision. Keep pressing until you reach your goal.

Greatness can only be obtained when you make up your mind that you will not compromise. As I mentioned previously, life will often try to make deals with you. Life will try to get you to give up on the pursuit of your dreams. You must realize that good isn't *good enough* when there is greatness within you. Don't settle for less when you were destined to have more. Establish what you want, when you want it, and how you are going to get it.

Be confident in who you are. Know that you have what it takes to reach your goals. You can desire

> *Greatness can only be obtained when you make up your mind that you will not compromise.*

to be the best of the best, have riches and fame, and have much success. However, it is essential that you hold firm to who you are, what you believe, and what you desire. Never compromise your values, goals and beliefs. It might get difficult and people may not always support you. You might even doubt yourself at times, but whatever you do, don't compromise.

Know Who You Are

One of the saddest things to witness is a person who has no sense of self-worth or appreciation. They often beat themselves up, accept failure, and find it hard to believe for anything greater than what they currently see. Their view of themselves is not one of high esteem. I want to remind you that everyone was created with a purpose and a plan, and it is this purpose that will help you discover your worth. Regardless of whether or not you look like the next person, have the same abilities or possess a lot of money, you are valuable. You matter. You are special.

You are made in the image of God. When you were created, it was in the best image. Therefore, you shouldn't settle for anything less than the best. There will never be another you. Therefore, embrace who you are, the gifts you have and the purpose for your life. When you embrace your gifts your value increases.

Abraham Lincoln said, "It is difficult to make a man miserable while he feels worthy of himself and claims kindred to the great God who made him." Once you have established your self-worth and realize that you were created in a special way, it will be extremely difficult to settle for less. The dreams that you have are too valuable for you to allow them to be diminished. Appreciate yourself. Celebrate yourself. Focus on the good qualities that you possess, and believe for nothing short of greatness for your life.

Stay Disciplined

Discipline allows you to remain fixed on your goal, despite the things that come to distract you. Regardless of what you are faced with, you must keep greatness at the forefront of your mind. Don't become distracted. Don't allow the perils of life to cause you to waiver in your pursuit of greatness. Moreover, fight the temptation to settle for less. It might be extremely difficult at times, but the reward will always outweigh the struggle.

Often when speaking to college students, I challenge them to embrace the attribute of discipline in their studies. I explain to them that they shouldn't allow television, peer pressure and pleasures not associated with their goals to allow them to become distracted. I even challenge them to shun whatever doesn't help them become successful in their desired pursuits. Often, as I make these statements, I notice some faces display inquisitive doubt, as if what I'm saying is wrong.

While I am not against having fun and enjoying the pleasures of life, I am against these things taking precedence over your purpose and dreams. Think about Mark Zuckerberg. While many of his peers were focused on partying and being socially accepted, Zuckerberg remained focused on his desire to connect to the world. His passion allowed him to display the discipline to not only create, but grow Facebook into a mammoth social tool, helping billions of people connect across the world. Facebook is now the largest social network in the world, and Zuckerberg has a net worth of over 30 billion dollars.

I am sure that Zuckerberg enjoyed social activities at times, and has many friends; however, neither of these "pleasures" distracted him from his purpose. Nor can you become so consumed with pleasure that you forgo your purpose. Muhammad Ali said, "I hated every minute of training, but I said, 'Don't quit. Suffer now and live the rest of your life as a champion.'" Sometimes, it will hurt to take a stand. It will often be painful to say no. However, in order for you to fulfill your purpose of greatness, discipline is an essential attribute to master.

IN IT TO WIN IT

In any form of competition, if you don't have the intention to win, competing is useless. Why engage in competition if you're not competing to win? Don't give up until you are victorious. In order to garner success, and to win in the game of life, you must be committed. Commitment is the ability to stick to the goal that you set out to accomplish long after the feeling in which you set the goal has left you.

It isn't uncommon that when you begin to set goals and have dreams that you become very excited. In fact, it is my desire that you become charged, motivated and inspired to be the great person you were born to be. However, what is most important is that you stay committed. When you face tough times, and run out of motivation, stick to the plan and the vision. This is the only way to reap the rewards of your labor.

Think about all of the people who set out to lose weight each year, or those who hope to give up smoking or profanity. Many charge out of the gates with joy and excitement, and they seem unstoppable. Unfortunately, few actually stick to their goal because they are not committed. If you are going to win in the game of life, it is imperative that you have more than emotional highs to keep you in the game.

Pain, happiness, laughter or sorrow—all of these emotions have the ability to change with each day. Therefore, your dreams can't be based solely on your emotions. They are manifested through work and commitment. Without commitment and actions toward your goals, all you will ever have is a lot of great thoughts and desires.

When you set out to tap into the greatness within, hard times are going to follow. But we know that the troubles that we face are meant to make us stronger. Greatness will always be confronted, but you must have a resolve that you won't give up. Decide that you will be great. Regardless of what happens or doesn't happen, decide to persevere and keep charging ahead. Think about this way—there is no need to oppose what isn't progressing. Therefore, if you are facing opposition, it means you're moving in the right direction.

Don't Go Back

In 2009, I had the opportunity to preach for the first time during a Sunday morning service. The message that I preached that day was, "Don't Go Back." That message is one that I will never forget. The message was centered on the story of Moses and the children of Israel as they traveled toward the land God promised them. These people endured much hardship and difficult times. All they wanted to become was inhabitants of the land that God had for them.

God gave the children of Israel the green light to enter into the land; however, they were to first

> *God will never give you a vision that you don't have the ability to bring to pass.*

go and scope out the land. They had to assess their future home and properly prepare for what was to come. Moses, the leader at the time, chose a small group to scope out the land. Everything that God promised would be in the land was there. However, they saw something that caused them to fear. They saw giants and perceived themselves as inferior to the giants. They doubted that they could inhabit the land that God promised them.

Most of the spies were fearful and doubtful that they could possess the land because of these giants. The fear was so real that it influenced the whole nation of people and caused them all to doubt. The people were so full of fear that many of them wanted to simply go back to where they had come from. However, Joshua and Caleb had a different thought. They believed that God would not bring them that far to let them be defeated by giants. They knew the victory was already won if they only believed.

God will never give you a vision that you don't have the ability to bring to pass. Furthermore, He would never make a promise to you that He would not bring to pass. Whatever you dream of or envision is possible if you're willing to believe in the abilities within.

The children of Israel failed to realize that they had everything they needed to make it. They overlooked the fact that God was with them, and that He led them to that place to give them the victory. They allowed the opinions and doubt of others to poison them and to lose sight of what God told them. Like Joshua and Caleb encouraged the children of Israel, I want to encourage you not to go back. You have come too far to give up. There is nothing behind you that can help move you to greatness. Keep moving forward and keep your eyes on the prize. Stay focused.

Remember Your Past Victories

Think about all the obstacles that you have overcome and the victories that you have won. Don't think for one second that they were coincidental. The greatness that you possess has been at work in your life all along. Your past triumphs should serve as an indication that you have the ability to win again and again. Your past struggles have set you up for future victories.

Maybe Joshua and Caleb were as confident as they were because they had seen God at work in their lives before. As Tye Tribbett said, "If He did it before, He will do it again. Same God right now, same God back then." In other words, if God was with you then, He will be with you now, regardless of what the situation looks like.

FINAL THOUGHT

It is certainly reassuring to know that the same power that worked within me in previous victories is still present today. We don't have to compromise, give up or lose faith in the possibility of greatness for our lives. Whenever faced with hard times, remember tough times don't last. The best is yet to come.

Unleashing your greatness can be difficult, and will often be confronted. However, you must resolve in your heart that you won't give up. You can both persevere and press past the pain, or you can allow it to stop you. Either way, the choice will be difficult; however, it will be more difficult to have to endure the pain associated with giving up. Keep pushing. You will gain a reward for the pain if you keep pushing.

9

THE POWER OF ATTITUDE
MAINTAINING A POSITIVE OUTLOOK

"Choosing to be positive and having a grateful attitude is going to determine how you're going to live your life." – Joel Osteen

Whenever I speak or write on the subject of attitude, I'm reminded of the saying, "Your attitude determines your altitude." Anyone who is honest with themselves knows this statement is very true. It is very unlikely that you will find a successful person, or anyone with sustained success, that has a negative attitude. Your attitude determines your quality of life. A positive attitude is essential in becoming great.

I view attitude in the same manner that I view tire pressure. If the tire pressure is too low, it can cause some serious problems. If the tire pressure is too low, the car struggles to gain as much traction as it could if the tire pressure was set correctly. Low tire pressure makes it more difficult to drive and steer. More power is required to pull the car, which affects gas mileage. If your gas mileage is affected, your wallet is affected. On the other hand, your tire pressure can be too high. Thus, you risk the chance of damaging your tires, and most notably could lead to a blowout. Too low or too high tire pressure can be life-threatening.

Having low tire pressure is indicative of a person with a low or negative attitude all the time. They're rarely motivated and they complain when they have to go above and beyond. This type of person brings down morale and affects the lives of everyone connected. No one wants to deal with this person. It's like having an extra load or carrying additional, unwanted baggage.

On the other side of the spectrum, the person who is always critical, nitpicky and angry is like a tire with too

Your attitude determines your quality of life. A positive attitude is essential in becoming great.

much pressure. This person is like a ticking time bomb. Everything upsets them. They are easily irritated and impatient. At any moment, they could blow. Therefore, a positive and healthy outlook is always necessary. Choosing to remain in good spirit with a positive attitude will cause you to go much further in life.

CHOOSE YOUR ATTITUDE

Everything that you want out of life begins with you. Make

the choice to become all that you want to become and have what you desire. You have the ability to choose how you will respond and react to certain situations. You determine the degree in which certain things affect you. Each week, I observe people on social media sites who post negative messages, expressing their discontentment with certain things in their lives. Furthermore, I've witnessed countless people who allow negativity to consume their outlook on life.

They come off as bitter, angry and troubled, often due to what was said or done to them by someone else. Somewhere in the minds of these individuals, they think that complaining about what they experienced will somehow make the situation better. In fact, often it only makes them more upset the more that they think about it. Complaining, murmuring and bickering about what is happening in your life will never change what happened. It won't change how you feel.

The only thing that will change how you feel about something is how you perceive it. This is where your attitude comes in. Instead of allowing things to bring you down, decide that it won't hinder you. Choose to see beyond your present circumstances and look toward a positive future.

In the book *Fish* by Stephen Lunden, Harry Paul and John Christensen one of the principles in the book is, *Choose Your Attitude*. What I personally gleaned from this principle was to rise above personal pain and drama, and focus on the task at hand. Focus on the task at hand in your life. Don't allow people or circumstances to cause you to become bitter when your objective is to become great.

Choosing your attitude is all about focus. Will you become distracted by something that perhaps isn't that important? Or will you remain focused on your goals? Will you allow opinions, negativity, doubt and fear to deflate you? Or will you remain locked in on what you have set out to do? Choosing your attitude will help you to remain even keeled. Like normal tire pressure, a good attitude will help you remain consistent and will help you get the most out of life.

Make the Best of Your Circumstances

Whether you are wealthy or poor, big, tall, skinny or short, whether you have multiple degrees or none at

> *The only thing that will change how you feel about something is how you perceive it.*

all, make the best of your circumstances. Perhaps you are at the top of your profession, or maybe you are just getting started. If you have failed at something, learn from it. If things are not working out the way that you planned, keep working because it will get better. We often find ourselves in positions that we didn't exactly ask for. It isn't what we would consider our ideal situation. But you can't allow that to affect your attitude.

You may be taking a class that you don't like. You may even be a part of the growing number of individuals that despise the jobs and careers that they have. Perhaps, you haven't yet realized the growth that you have been working so hard for. There is a way to handle your discomforts. Use the class that you don't enjoy as an opportunity to grow and learn. The job that you don't enjoy is nothing more than a stepping stone to something better. For those of you that are experiencing slow growth, use this time to make sure that everything is in order so that when growth begins to happen, you'll be ready and prepared for such success. But you must keep a positive attitude.

Your situations don't have to get the best of you. Things will get better for you. You will make more money, you will become successful and you will experience happiness and joy on levels that you have never experienced before. All of your success hinges upon your ability to cope with the unpleasant situations that you're facing right now. Although you may find yourself in undesirable situations, greatness is often birthed out of these predicaments. It is in these times of affliction that we discover how powerful we truly are.

Be Grateful

I am thoroughly convinced that no matter how bad a person's situation might be, there is someone that is in a worse position. The things that we consider to be burdens could be blessings to someone else. The job that you complain about is a blessing to someone that is unemployed and living without consistent income. When you complain about your spouse getting on your last nerve, remember that there is someone who wishes that they were married. You may not have everything that you want right now. You may not have reached some of the goals that you have set, but understand that things could be worse.

When you are grateful for what you have and begin to count your blessings, you will be more appreciative. This attitude will cause you to be much

> *You can have the life that you want to have as long as you're willing to maintain the attitude necessary to help you get that life.*

more diligent and faithful over what you have, and will cause you to get the most out of what you have. As Joel Osteen said, "Choosing to be positive and having a grateful attitude is going to determine how you're going to live your life." You can have the life that you want to have as long as you're willing to maintain the attitude necessary to help you get that life.

FINAL THOUGHT

Unless you learn to be grateful, choose a positive attitude, and make the best of your circumstances, greatness will always elude you. In order to be great, you cannot neglect the necessity of a good attitude. A negative attitude will only subtract from your life. On the other hand, a positive attitude will aid you in unleashing the greatness within. Therefore, whenever you find yourself wrestling with negative thoughts, remember these words: "Fix your thoughts on what is true, and honorable, and right, and pure, and lovely, and admirable. Think about things that are excellent and worthy of praise" (Phil. 4:8-9 ESV).

10

THE POWER OF CHANGE
CHANGE IS NECESSARY

"Be the change that you wish to see in the world."
– Mahatma Gandhi

Change can be good or bad. It all depends on your perception. However, those who are committed to unleashing their inner greatness should embrace change and see it as a vital piece in the puzzle of greatness. I have learned to embrace change. Change can always yield something positive in your life. You may have suffered a loss of a loved one or lost a job. You may have been diagnosed with an adverse health condition. You might even constantly find yourself disadvantaged. No matter the situation, change *can* be good.

Despite the circumstances at hand, your attitude determines how you handle it. Remember your attitude is key. Change is inevitable; you can't avoid it. Nothing stays the same. The world is constantly evolving, progressing and changing. Those that will survive the vicissitudes of life are those who will embrace change and learn to see the good in all situations.

The Importance of Change

In 2008, Illinois State Senator and Presidential Candidate, Barak Obama, burst on the political scene with a simple message: *Change*. He had garnered much support and notoriety with this simple, yet catchy campaign slogan. His message was clear: change was needed and change had come. Prior to Obama running for office, the nation was in economic and social ruin. People lost hope and faith in our government, and even doubted humanity as a whole. Obama made it clear to the people of the United States of America that things would be different if he were elected.

Obama was elected as the President of the United States, becoming the 44th President and the first ever African-American President of our nation. While some believe much has changed since his election into office, others believe not so much. I am not here to debate nor defend Obama's political resume. I simply want to point out how his message of change signified something that we all yearn for. His political experience can teach us a few things. Most importantly, it reveals to us that change is necessary.

No matter who you are, when things are going bad, you want them to get better. Furthermore, when things are good, we desire

> *Change is inevitable; you can't avoid it. Nothing stays the same. The world is constantly evolving, progressing and changing.*

something even greater. Change is necessary if you're going to thrive in this life. If you want to see growth and betterment, you have to learn to adapt.

Looking at President Obama's tenure reveals many things. Whether you support Obama or not, his time in office has revealed to us a few things:

1. *Change is necessary.*

Beyond that which I have previously mentioned, change reveals the need for action. You might be one who believes that Obama has failed as President. However, even in Obama's failures, we can see the things that are needed to be done in order to not repeat the same failures. The actions needed to become better are more clearly defined, which perhaps may not have been so without some setbacks. Despite some people's issue with Obama, it was necessary for him to be President. Moreover, it was necessary for him to have some setbacks to clearly define what change is needed going forward.

The same goes for us. Even in times of struggles and setbacks, we can learn what adjustments are needed in our lives. Change is necessary if we're ever going to tap into our greatness. We can't expect greatness if we refuse to accept change.

2. *Learn from it.*

When Obama came into office, there were things that his predecessors did that he used as invaluable teaching aids. While he may not have always known what to do, he often knew what *not* to do. In his time in office thus far, Obama has made mistakes, and he has celebrated victories. When his tenure as President is over, the next President of the United States will learn from Obama.

Life isn't perfect, and every day will not be sunny. You will have setbacks and disappointments. Instead of allowing them to defeat you, learn from them. Allow the happenings in your life to help you make the necessary adjustments to reach full greatness. Success and failure are two of the greatest teachers. You cannot change what you are ignorant of.

3. *Embrace change.*

There were many people who did not want Obama to become President. There were some who felt that he was too young, while others simply liked the other candidates better. Perhaps you didn't want him to become President because you are Republican and he's a Democrat. You may have been one of those who rejected him based on his skin color, religious views and family history. Nevertheless, those views didn't change the course of history.

While many rejected his point of change, it didn't stop change from happening.

Things don't go your way all of the time. You have the choice and the ability to make the necessary adjustments to better your situation. I like something my friend DeAndre Carter said, "Learn to use your irritation to increase your inspiration." Instead of fighting change and allowing it to make you resentful, use it to inspire you to make a difference and a positive impact in the world.

4. Be the change.

For many of Obama's supporters it was believed that he embodied the change that the nation needed. In many instances Obama was forefront in igniting the change that he desired to see in our world. Likewise, you must be the catalyst for the things that you want to happen in your life. If you want a better career, you have to work for it. If you want a successful marriage, strive toward being a great spouse. Whatever you desire, you have to put forth the effort to make it happen. Furthermore, when you see the many problems in our society—failed school systems, troubled youth and an unstable economy—contribute to the betterment of these things! Don't sit back idly and watch the world go by. Get up, and make your mark on the world.

In the past, I've discussed certain concerns about church and ministry with my pastor. There were a lot of things that I had expressed to him in displeasure. But during these times he always challenged me to do something about it. My problem was that instead of actually working to make a difference, I grew critical and consumed by what I saw and didn't agree with. I quickly had to accept that change begins with me. You too must accept that change begins within. What you work to fix within will eventually be revealed externally. You can't expect to change if you have not changed on the inside.

Oftentimes, the problems that you have are not with others or your situation. The problem is within you. Take the focus off of everything and everyone else, and focus on yourself. When we focus on ourselves and not the problem, we will find the solution for many of the world's issues. Mirror the image that you want to see in this world. If you want to improve the state of our society, become a better citizen. Be the change that you hope to see in the world. No matter how minor or great your impact is, it does make a difference.

FINAL THOUGHT

Change is necessary and inevitable. Furthermore, change begins with you. It is necessary for you to change, grow and evolve if you're ever going to experience true greatness. No matter how uncomfortable and unpleasant change can be, you must accept it. Take the time to make the necessary adjustments to live a life of impact. Never shun the opportunity to change and grow because you view your actions as minor. Every minor action has the ability to yield major results. Tap into the greatness within, and remember change is inevitable. Embrace it. Learn from it.

11

THE POWER OF SERVICE
THE GREATEST AMONG US

"Service is the price that you pay for the space that you occupy."
– Dr. Dennis Kimbro

In a world full of people who are self-seeking and selfish, the idea of being selfless might be foreign to some. Many people seek what others can do for them instead of questioning what they can do to better someone else's quality of life. President John F. Kennedy said, "Ask not what your country can do for you, but ask what you can do for your country." As JFK delivered this speech, he may have had the thought in mind that in order for us to advance as a nation, we must embrace the idea of thinking about someone other than ourselves. It is imperative that we understand that in seeking to do for others, we open the doors for endless possibilities.

Where would the world be without people who are willing to give of themselves to help aid in the betterment of someone else? Imagine going to a restaurant and not having a waiter to assist you. Imagine a world without bus drivers, taxi drivers, airplane pilots or train conductors. How would you travel? Without these people, and so many others like them who have committed their lives to service, our lives would be much more difficult. Service is an essential driving force in our society.

Anyone can serve. We all have something that we can give that can help make someone else's life easier.

...we must embrace the idea of thinking about someone other than ourselves.

Remember that there is greatness within you. However, that greatness requires that you share it with others. It is essentially the price that you must pay for the gift that you have been given.

The Way to Greatness

One of the most thought-provoking sayings of Jesus is, *The greatest among you must be a servant* (Matt. 23:11 NLT). Why would Jesus connect being a servant to being great? Understand that it takes a special person to serve. A servant possesses qualities that few on this earth are willing to embrace. They must be patient, selfless, understanding and loving. Servants normally help make someone else's life more pleasant and comfortable while being placed in a position that isn't so desirable for themselves.

Society teaches that those who serve are inferior. Servants aren't widely respected. Furthermore, they are often underappreciated and underpaid. However, most of those who have "arrived" more than likely at some point found themselves being servants. The surest and most honest way to the top is to embrace the qualities of servitude. You can't expect to be served if you aren't willing to serve others.

Regardless of our income, educational level, or social class, we should all seek to have the heart of a servant. Therefore, whether or not you are just starting out on your journey to greatness, or you are living out your dreams, be passionate and thankful for the opportunity to serve. For those who are striving toward greatness, keep pushing forward.

> *The surest and most honest way to the top is to embrace the qualities of servitude.*

Your service will pave the way to success. If you're already living your dreams, keep serving because your service sustains your success and ultimately, makes someone else's life better.

Steve Jobs wanted to make the quality of life of others better. Jobs, along with a group of friends set out to revolutionize the computer, not to make themselves rich, but to better humanity. Steve Jobs said, "Being the richest man in the cemetery doesn't matter to me. Going to bed at night saying we've done something wonderful... that's what matters to me." It was this mentality that allowed him to ultimately become great, and what opened many doors for him.

Service Opens Doors for You

One of my mentors and success coach, Ken Brown, has a phenomenal story. His testimony shows how servitude makes great things happen for you. After graduating college, he had a tough time landing that dream job. Therefore, he had to somewhat settle for a job that didn't quite meet his expectations. He became a waiter at one of the top restaurants in Detroit. What he did after taking the job is what set him apart from many of his peers and colleagues. Instead of complaining and murmuring about how this wasn't the job that he wanted, or acting as if being a waiter was beneath him, he embraced the opportunity to serve. He was committed to excellence and great service. He decided that he would not let his paycheck dictate his work ethic. He gave it his all.

Ken Brown modeled this principle, "Work as unto the Lord, and not unto man" in his daily affairs. It was his strong work ethic, consistency and faith that something greater would come from that opportunity that ultimately got him noticed by a top-ranking executive of McDonald's. This woman was eventually instrumental in him opening his first two McDonald's restaurants. Now a millionaire entrepreneur, speaker and author, Ken Brown can attest to the fact that service opens doors for you. Looking at his story, Ken Brown used service as a down payment on living out his dreams.

I like something that Dr. Dennis Kimbro mentions in his book, *The Wealth Choice: Success Secrets of Black Millionaires.* He mentions an equation regarding service. The equation is:

$$Q+Q+MA = C$$

This means the *quality* of your service, plus the *quantity* of your service, plus the *mental attitude* that you do it in determines your *compensation.* The equation argues that people can make you rich or broke by the way that you treat them. Much like the saying, "*you reap what you sow.*" The harvest that you will receive is indicative of the seeds that you have sown.

Dr. Dennis Kimbro said, "Service is the price you pay for the space that you occupy." In life, you have been given time, space and opportunity to make a difference. You can be anything that you desire to become, but the fulfillment of the desire comes with a price. That price is service.

Everything that you do should represent the necessary steps to take you where you desire to go. Regardless of what your status is

> *People can make you rich or broke by the way that you treat them.*

in society, learn to embrace small, seemingly unimportant things in life. It's rare to witness people who want to serve and make a difference in the lives of others these days. Many people just want to be served.

When was the last time you did something for someone with no strings attached? When was the last time you went beyond your comfort zone to make someone else comfortable? This is the ultimate key to success. When you can learn to be self-sacrificing and unselfish, your actions reciprocate back to you in abundant satisfaction and joy.

The greatest in our society are those who recognize that servitude equates to success. How you serve will determine how far you will go in life. If you want greater, you must be willing to give. Doors will open for you, or doors will shut in your face. The direction of the doors all depends on your ability to serve someone other than yourself.

Serve God and Serve Others

It can be challenging to adopt the idea that the greatest among us must be servants. Our society is full of people who regard serving as being "less than" or inferior. When I look at the servant, I've found that they exhibit strength and resiliency. In order to serve, you must have the desire to make a difference. Furthermore, you must have patience and fortitude. You must also be selfless and willing to give. With those attributes, what Jesus suggests makes sense.

It is my relationship with God that allows me to serve others so willingly. God is giving, caring and compassionate. These attributes of God stir the desire within me to make a difference. I don't buy into the notion that God is this fire-breathing being that is out to get you whenever you fall short. I view Him as a Father that simply wants the best for His children, and will teach, reward and discipline you in an attempt to make sure you get the best out of life. When you serve God, you can't help but change lives through the true power of service.

Do Unto Others

The golden rule simply states, "Do unto others as you would have them do unto you." In short, treat others how you want to be treated. This is a simple, yet complex principle. If you value and love yourself, and don't want anyone to hurt or devalue you, you should want to avoid doing that to someone else. However, it is difficult for those who are selfish, uncompassionate beings. Many people think that pushing, loving or supporting someone else will somehow decrease their opportunities for better. Instead, we should help, love and encourage one another. We should seek to find ways to better someone else's life around us. There is nothing wrong with wanting success and opportunity, but let's not get so clouded with our own desires that we lose sight of everyone else's needs.

One of the saddest things to witness for me is the "crab in the bucket mentality." Instead of helping someone else out of the bucket, many would much rather claw away at someone else's dreams and goals, believing that somehow, this might give them an edge in reaching their own goals. However, I like the idea that my friend, Antoine D. Jackson, presents in his book, *100 Watt Life*. He said, "Just because I shine my light doesn't mean that I, in any way, diminish your light from shining." When we both shine, we make things brighter. Therefore, be helpers one to another, and assist those in need.

Putting Yourself in Their Shoes

How would you feel if someone was trying to put out your flame while you're attempting to pursue your greatness? I

There is nothing wrong with wanting success and opportunity, but let's not get so clouded with our own desires that we lose sight of everyone else's needs.

am sure that you would neither enjoy nor appreciate someone doing that. Furthermore, how would you feel if someone labeled or judged you without proper knowledge of who you really are?

Some people claim they don't care what others think of them, and that's fine. But no one likes to deal with those haters; you know, those dream killers I talked about previously. When people tear others down, they fail to consider how the person they are tearing down feels. Maybe they don't care, but they neglect how they might feel if the tables were turned.

One thing I admire most about the ministry of Jesus is His compassion. The love that Jesus exhibited to those that He came in contact with is something that should be noted. One of the greatest examples of this is when Jesus was faced with a woman who was caught in adultery. Many people shunned this woman for her sin and they wanted to hear what Jesus had to say concerning the matter. Furthermore, they wanted to stone the woman, as the law at that time commanded. However, Jesus turned the tables and had the people place themselves in her shoes. He tells them simply, *"Let the one who has never sinned throw the first stone"* (John 8:7 NLT). The people in the multitude had to put themselves in a position that caused them to take inventory of their own faults.

Although there is greatness within you, we all have flaws and shortcomings. Likewise, you should be compassionate and caring for others who have flaws. Therefore, learn to help, encourage and appreciate others. Instead of being critical, be caring and kind. Become a servant to others; assisting them to become great.

FINAL THOUGHT

Embrace the concept of servitude and selflessness by recognizing that we all need each other. The world would be most miserable if we all neglected the necessity of serving. In serving, doors will open for you. What you make happen for someone else, God makes happen for you. The greatest people in this world are those who serve.

12

THE POWER OF RELATIONSHIPS
MAKING THE RIGHT CONNECTIONS

"Two people are better off than one, for they can help each other succeed. If one person falls, the other can reach out and help. But someone who falls alone is in real trouble."
- Ecclesiastes 4:9-10 NLT

Unfortunately, there are too many people in the world who believe that they can be a "one man show." They somehow believe that success can be obtained alone. I often hear individuals quote, after they've acquired much success, "I pulled myself up by my own boot straps." This is foolishness. The boot straps that one claims to have pulled themselves up by were made by someone else. If not, the material that made up the boot straps came from someone else's effort. The point is, we all depend on the efforts of others. We all need each other. Relationships are a vital component in the greatness equation. It may not be completely impossible to have *some* success on your own. But you will never achieve greatness by yourself. You may have heard, "Teamwork makes the dream work." Growing a business, winning a championship and raising children are much easier with teamwork. Unfortunately, there are some who seek success on their own accord. There are many who believe that they can be great based on their singular effort and ability. You may be able to accomplish a lot on your own, but you will need the assistance of others to unleash your full potential and greatness.

Like the wise man said, *"Two are better than one."* It is much better to have assistance while pursuing your goals and dreams than to go at it alone. Your greatness is often dependent on the relationships and connections that you make. Your connections ultimately serve as a major indicator in whether or not you will be successful.

I Need You to be Great

There are vital connections that you need in order to fulfill your purpose. Without Judas, Jesus could not have fulfilled his purpose of dying for humanity. Without Steve Wozniak, there would be no Steve Jobs, and Apple wouldn't be as successful as it is today. In addition, without competition, many companies or individuals would never realize their potential and greatness.

There are two things that we need to understand. First, there are certain people that we need in our lives in order for our goals to be accomplished. Secondly, competition is necessary for us to achieve the level of greatness meant for us. We must be surrounded by the right people in order to truly discover the greatness that is within.

Proverbs 27:17 (NIV) says, *As iron sharpens iron, so one person sharpens another*. Michael Jordan

It is much better to have assistance while pursuing your goals and dreams than to go at it alone.

admits that his battles with the Detroit Pistons helped make him the player that the world has come to know. Companies like Ford, Chrysler and General Motors are constantly competing against each other, attempting to gain an edge in the automotive industry. Walt Disney said, "I have been up against tough competition all my life. I wouldn't know how to get along without it." Healthy competition among others is a valuable asset in obtaining your level of desired success. Essentially, it is iron sharpening iron. The connections that you make, as well as the competition that you face, is like fuel for greatness. Surround yourself with people that can help you reach your goals and bring out the best in you.

The Right Team

Someone once asked Michael Jordan in an interview who he thought the best player in the NBA was. He said, "It's not about who the best player is; it's about the best team." The best player is only as good as the team that he plays for. Your support system plays a great role in solidifying the greatness within. Consider NBA players Kevin Garnett and Lebron James. Each of these players are incredible athletes with immense skill and ability.

Kevin Garnett, for many years, played for the Minnesota Timberwolves. Throughout that span his team made numerous playoff appearances. They came close on multiple occasions to winning the NBA championship. However, the team never prevailed over their opponents. It was not until Garnett joined the Boston Celtics that he became an NBA champion. In Boston, he linked up with players who shared his same passion and reasoning. He was a part of the right team.

Lebron James has a similar story. James came closer on more occasions than Garnett did, yet still couldn't obtain the prize. When James joined the Miami Heat, along with Chris Bosh and Dwayne Wade, the dream of becoming a champion would finally become a reality. James had the right team.

With the right team, anything is possible. On the other hand, without the right people in place, success is much more difficult and often out of reach. Van Moody teaches the importance and power of relationships in his book, *The People Factor*. He urges that relationships can help push you to where you want to be, or hinder your progress.

Therefore, it is essential that you assess current and future relationships. While you shouldn't be skeptical

> *Assess the relationships in your life to properly place each relationship in its respective place. Doing so will benefit you and those connected to you greatly.*

of everyone that you come in contact with, you should be mindful of people that aren't adding to your vision. They may not be hurting you, but they are not helping you. You may notice that there are people in your life who supposedly add no benefit. However, before casting them off determine if you are supposed to be a benefit to them. All relationships are not for our personal gain. You never know how your vision, efforts and wisdom may help someone else become better.

Assess the relationships in your life to properly place each relationship in its respective place. Doing so will benefit you and those connected to you greatly.

The Most Important Relationship

You may believe that the greatest relationship that one could have is with a spouse, or perhaps the relationship between a child and their parents. However, the most important relationship that any of us can have is a relationship with God. Greatness is only made possible through a relationship with Him.

Greatness cannot be fully obtained until you have a connection with the one who planted greatness within you. James 1:17 tell us that, *Every good and perfect give comes from above...* Therefore, the greatness that we possess; the power, potential, and the gifts all come from God. God is our teacher, our coach, our Father, the one who will show us how to properly maximize our greatness.

The biggest secret to unleashing your greatness is to recognize that it is, *In Him (God) we live and move and have our being* (Acts 17: 28 ESV). Some may argue that greatness is possible without acknowledging or serving God. While there are many who have accomplished great things without acknowledging God, the fullest potential will only be accomplished from having that connection with God.

How much greater could a person be if they used their gifts for God, the one who gave them the gifts in the first place? We must all strive to make a

> *Greatness cannot be fully obtained until you have a connection with the one who planted greatness within you.*

difference with the amount of greatness granted to us. This is our God-given purpose and responsibility. I would have never accomplished half of what I've accomplished thus far, nor would I be the man I am today without God and my relationship with Jesus Christ. Like me, there are countless people who share these exact sentiments.

The Apostle Paul, who was formerly Saul of Tarsus, was always regarded as an esteemed and respectable figure in his community. However, it wasn't until he had an experience with Christ that he realized his true calling, potential and purpose—and ultimately, his greatness. Throughout much of his writings, Paul attributes his success to God. Furthermore, many modern examples—athletes, actors and artists credit their success to God. There is no denying that God is our greatest help to unleash the greatness within. There is no doubt that the most important relationship anyone can have is with God.

FINAL THOUGHT

The biggest key is to realize that no one is here by their own accord and effort. We need each other, and we need God. If we were designed to make it on our own, relationships wouldn't play such a vital part in our daily lives. There indeed is power in relationships. Be sure that you are forming and sustaining the right relationships. Without them, greatness doesn't exist.

13

THE POWER OF INFLUENCE
INSPIRE. INFORM. INSTRUCT. IMPACT.

"The purpose behind everything that I do is to inspire, inform, instruct, and ultimately, make an impact." – DeAndre Riley

Inspire, Inform, Instruct, Impact. This is the foundation upon which my business was established, and it is the slogan that I live by in my daily life. Furthermore, through the principles outlined in this book, it is my desire that you will become inspired. I want you to be informed, as well as gain instruction, and ultimately become impacted to be great. Moreover, I pray that you will in turn take the challenge to do the same for others. I have no doubt that when we were created, we were created with the ability to do this. Whenever I get the opportunity to speak with a group of individuals, I always attempt to make this point very plain. I believe that we are all people of influence. I believe that we all can be difference makers.

There is power in using your influence to make a difference. In fact, using your influence to impact people in a

> *...using your influence to impact people in a positive way is the epitome of greatness.*

positive way is the epitome of greatness. Influence is simply the ability to persuade, motivate or move someone. In short, influence is the power to make things happen. During the remainder of this chapter, I will explain how we can utilize the power of influence through my business slogan: *Inspire, Inform, Instruct and Impact.*

INSPIRE

Inspiration is the foundation of influence. We are all influential, whether we believe it or not. It was author Scott Adams that said, "You don't have to be a person of influence to be influential. In fact, the most influential people in my life are probably not even aware of the things they've taught me." In other words, you don't have to be the president or CEO. You don't have to be a millionaire or famous to inspire others.

Whether you know it or not, many of you reading this book constantly influence and inspire people, but are often oblivious to it. Someone is watching you. You are teaching the world something. Your life is a reflection of what you are teaching the world. Make the most of it.

Make up your mind that you are going to be a difference maker. Decide that you will use your time and life to be committed to helping others become better. In your own personal journey of greatness, don't forget the responsibility that we have in assisting others with the same goal. Therefore, be selfless and giving by using your influence toward the betterment of others. In addition, I want you to ask yourself these basic questions:

1. *What am I passionate about?*

2. *What am I good at? What are my gifts?*

3. *How can I help someone in need?*

How you answer these questions will reveal to you how you can ultimately be an inspiration.

Your Passion

It is vital that you define your passion. Your passion is often directly tied to your purpose and calling in life. Furthermore, your passion is the fuel that drives you toward your goals. Oprah Winfrey said, "Passion is energy. Feel the power that comes from focusing on what excites." You have identified your passion when you can do that thing with no expectation of reward. Just the mere thought of your passion excites you. My passion is speaking. Speaking that makes a difference and invokes change is my primary joy and desire. Therefore, whether I am preaching to a congregation or teaching principles to staff and leadership, my passion is to see people changed.

Some people say you must make your passion your play. If you do, you will never have to work again. The passion that you possess toward certain things brings about an immediate excitement and satisfaction just at the mere thought of it. Living a life of passion is gratifying and fulfilling. Whether anyone praises, pays or promotes you, your disposition never falters. Your passion is the one thing that will cause you to always remain consistent, confident and focused. If you can identify your passion, you have identified your purpose and calling. That is the first step in helping you inspire others to pull greatness from within.

Your Gift

A gift is that thing that you can do with much ease, something that is simply second nature to you. Some people are just gifted or born with the ability to do what they currently do. The greatest singers, athletes, actors and entrepreneurs all possess the gifting to do what they do so successfully. While it is definitely hard work that gets results, hard work only produces the results that the gift yields. It still takes skills and gifts, along with hard work to excel in your purpose and passion.

While we are all born with gifts and talents, what separates many from success and failure are those who take that gift and mix it with faith, hard work and passion. Your gift, when mixed with your passion, will open many doors for you. In addition, your gift will drive you to purpose fulfillment and greatness. Your gift will make room for you and bring you before great men and opportunities.

However, understand that your gift comes with immense responsibility. Find your gift. Find your passion and accompany those things with character, selflessness and purpose. You are responsible for doing the work required to make your gift and passion work. Your gift is your "it factor." It is your proverbial key to success. What will separate the successful from the unsuccessful is the fact that one group uses that gift to make a difference and inspire, while another group uses their gift in selfish pursuits, never taking the time to inspire others.

Filling the Need

Once you pinpoint what your passion and gifts are, you have to identify how you will use them. The best way to determine this is to fill a need. Like Zuckerberg who used Facebook to fill the desire for people to be connected, and Steve Jobs who desired to see a more people-friendly PC, you must take your gifts and passions and utilize them to make a difference in the world.

When you set out to inspire and transform lives, your reach will expand into other things. Not only will your reach grow, but you will grow as a person. The greatest amount of satisfaction can be found in knowing that you made a difference in someone else's life. There is no greater feeling for me than to know that it was something that I said or did that motivated someone to do something or become better. I saw a need to help people discover their greatness; therefore, I wrote this book. Not only did I help others become great, but I have also grown. I saw a need and I filled it.

Being Inspired

Like a water pitcher that is constantly used, you have to take a moment to be refilled. This is why Christians attend church weekly, professionals attend workshops and seminars, and teachers are constantly sharpening their educational tools. When you constantly pour out, you have to stop and refuel. Be open to learning new things. Get to know different people. Stretch yourself. Expand your mind to new possibilities. Most importantly, be appreciative of those around you who have been placed in your life to help you become better. Sometimes, the greatest inspiration can come in the smallest forms.

I have learned to immerse myself wholly into what I hope to become. As a speaker, I watch speakers who are already successful. As a preacher and minister, I have devoted hours and years to studying and understanding the Word of God. As an entrepreneur, I am constantly sharpening my tools, trying to gain a competitive edge.

Therefore, I consistently attend workshops and seminars that will help me become a better entrepreneur. I believe the saying, "By beholding, you become changed." By watching and learning from the examples of others who have done what you may be trying to accomplish, you are sure to enhance your chances of operating in greatness.

There's a quote that says, "You are only as good as the top five people that you hang around." In essence, this saying lends to the idea that those who you associate yourself with will influence what type of life you live. It's like the old adage, "Birds of a feather flock together." Your surroundings and the company you keep help paint a picture for your future reality. I learned after much setback, disappointment and failures that if I was going to be successful in any area, I had to surround myself with people that would help me become successful. I recognized that I couldn't be a successful student, entrepreneur, author, speaker or Christian without surrounding myself with positive influences.

You must open yourselves up to new possibilities and realities. In order to have something different, you must see different things. Since I'm from the eastside of Detroit, at times, this has been extremely difficult. There is no shortage of blight, crime and failure in Detroit. However, there are a lot of great things about Detroit. I made a decision. I could focus on the negativity, or I could seek the positive things that the city has to offer. Therefore, I choose to focus on personal, professional and spiritual development. I choose to focus on positive things that aid me in being great.

Inspiration is all around us. It is so important that we tap into it in order to be influential to others and ourselves. It is

> *Your surroundings and the company you keep help paint a picture for your future reality.*

because of the inspiration that I received from so many that I am able to do what I do today. Find inspiration to push you to your greatness.

INFORM & INSTRUCT

Information brings transformation. When you lack knowledge, you miss opportunities for growth and development. Therefore, when you know better, you will do better. It is imperative that we stay in a continual state of learning if we are going to continue to grow and get better. We have to stretch ourselves and see life from different perspectives. We have to be informed.

To learn is to grow. Learning gives us life. In fact, it was William Burroughs that said, "The moment you stop learning, you start dying." Nothing is worse than missing out on growth, life and betterment because you lacked the knowledge to get there.

The Danger in Not Learning

Ignorance will keep you idle. Ignorance will limit you and cause you not to tap into the potential that you have within. You will never reach the heights of success in certain areas without proper knowledge and being well informed. Look at people like doctors, real estate agents and other licensed professionals. They have to undergo, in many instances, a required learning structure to maintain their professional licenses called continuing education. They are expected to obtain so many credit hours in order to maintain their status, or else they cannot continue to practice in their field. They are held accountable to stay current with the knowledge needed for them to properly do their jobs. If they are going to become or remain successful, knowledge is key.

Everyone claims that they want more and want to do more, yet very few actually take the steps necessary to fulfill those desires. As I previously stated, it isn't enough to just want or believe for something. You have to put forth some action in order to make things happen. Faith without works is dead.

Faith is what you are believing for, but the works is the knowledge applied to get what you believe. That's why I like the quote that says, "You don't get out of life what you want. You get out of life who you are." This quote speaks volumes. It implies that you must become what you hope to attract. Like a magnet attracts other metals, you have to become what you want to attract. Knowledge and information bridges the gap between what you desire and what you receive. However, if you remain ignorant, you will never reach your goals.

Be Teachable

One of the hardest things for any of us to digest is that we don't have all of the answers. None of us can make it on our own. We all need what someone else has to offer in order to make it. I had to learn to stop trying to control everything, realizing that I can do better with the help of others. I had to open myself up to learn from others. I learned that in doing radio, I needed to seek the knowledge and experience of others to help me to build and brand my broadcast properly. In speaking, I learned that there are clues that many successful speakers leave that helped them become successful. Furthermore, I hired a success coach to help me define my goals and implement strategies to help me become successful. I had to become teachable.

If we desire greatness and hope to ever unleash it, we have to be informed and instructed on how to do so. I don't claim to have all the answers; therefore, I expect that after reading this book, you will continue to learn and grow. I hope what you learn here will ignite an even greater hunger for knowledge. Remain teachable and be open to learn new things.

Applying What You've Learned

As we interface with people and are placed in various situations, applying the knowledge will help us navigate through these experiences. Once you gain knowledge, you have the responsibility to share that knowledge. You now must become the instructor. Again, you may not have all of the answers, but there is knowledge and wisdom that can be shared to help others. However, all too often, I have witnessed people of social, religious, political and educational esteem shun and profane those who have fallen short in the many areas in which they themselves have succeeded.

People are often quick to criticize the young girl who got pregnant at a young age. They are quick to ridicule the young man who has broken the law or dropped out of school. Oftentimes, we are critical of people that seemingly are the opposite of who we are and who we aspire to become. But, what have you done to help them? Have you instructed people on how to conduct themselves? If you're not part of the solution, you may be part of the problem.

Many have a wealth of experience and knowledge to offer those in need. Some of us have so many resources and connections that we can offer to others to help them excel. When you encounter people who are not living up to their potential, understand that something can be done to help them reach their full potential— but it all begins with you. You can assist someone. You can instruct and share your experiences to help point people in the right direction. The information that you receive is most effective when you share it with those who need it.

Life will present us all with circumstances that can handicap and limit us. It is knowledge and instruction that helps us overcome these limits. You don't have to reinvent the wheel or chart a new path in order to make it happen. Simply follow the examples of the countless individuals that have gone before you and learn from them. Like the saying goes, *"success leaves clues."*

IMPACT

The purpose in serving as an inspiration for others, the purpose in informing and instructing others is so that we

> *Greatness is only defined by the impact that you have on others.*

can have an impact. Greatness is only defined by the impact that you have on others. Therefore, without making a mark in the world, your greatness is void. Greatness isn't about what can be done for you; it's about what you do for others. How much you gain and prosper means nothing if you haven't helped someone else prosper.

In all that we do, our intentions should be to use our God-given gifts and talents to impact the world in a positive way. Be inspired. Be an inspiration. Continue to seek knowledge while informing and instructing others. When we practice these principles, and hold dear to them, there is no doubt that we will be great.

Epilogue

It is my most sincere prayer and desire that you have become empowered—empowered to build, empowered to grow, and empowered to be great in all areas of your life. Allow the principles outlined in this book to serve as a blueprint or game plan of sorts to help you unleash the greatness within. I challenge you to see yourself better, wiser and stronger than before. Remember, you are powerful, gifted and talented. Greatness is within you and the best is yet to come.

I challenge you to commit daily to helping others unleash the greatness within them. Whether you know it or not, your life will never serve its greatest purpose except you endeavor to help make someone else great. Regardless of how great you are, the true extent of your greatness is realized in sharing that greatness with others. Therefore, refuse to be idle. Refrain from being selfish and self-seeking. Find out what you can do to better the world. The world will thank you for it.

Finally, I say thank you for trusting me with your time and for purchasing this book. It means everything to me that you have shared this experience with me. Encourage others to get this book, and share your feedback with your network, family and friends. This is my gift to the world, and I hope that you will help me share it. Blessings to you and yours!

DeAndre M. Riley - "D.R. Speaks"

ACKNOWLEDGMENTS

This is the one portion of the book that is very personal to me. Whether you as a reader ever read this portion, it is important for me to honor and thank those who have helped me get to where I am today. I recognize that without the help of the many people that have poured into my life, I would be nothing. There are literally hundreds of people that I can thank right now. However, time would fail me to do so.

I first would like to thank my Lord and Savior Jesus Christ. I can be great because you made yourself of no reputation, taking my place on Calvary's cross. *"Because He lives, I can live again."*

To my wife Porsha,

On January 28, 2012, our lives changed forever. We became one, and I thank God He that He allowed me to find you. I can truly say that I am favored of the Lord to have you as my life partner, best friend and companion. You accepted me, flaws and all, and helped to bring out the best in me. Thank you for your unconditional love and dedication to me and always being there to encourage me when I get down. Thank you for your patience with me in this endeavor, and thank you for always believing in me. The best is yet to come. There will be many more books where I will mention you in appreciation. I am excited about our future, and believe that greater things await us. Of course, my excitement grew when I found out that we were expecting, and that in March 2015, we will be welcoming D.R Speaks Jr. to the world.

To my grandparents,

I am sure that when you planned out your life, it probably didn't include taking in five children after the loss of your third child, my mother. However, my siblings and I are forever indebted to you in that you sacrificed so much so that we could stay together as a family. I did not always appreciate your sacrifices as a child, but as I grow older, I am reminded every day of your undying love for your family. Thank you for all that you have done. I will never forget it.

To my siblings,

David (April), DaJuan, Dion (Eutopia), Danita (Stephen), Dawn, Juanetta, and Keanda (Eric): It sure is a lot of us. We all range in age, some of us have different fathers, and some have different mothers, but we are one family. I love each of you, and I am blessed to be your brother. We've been through the fire, but I thank God none of us smell like smoke. You would never know by the way we smile and carry out our daily lives that we have been through the things we've been through. But what didn't kill us, made us stronger. I pray that through my life, I can inspire each of you to greater things. I love you all. Let's change the world together.

To my first born, Serenity Michelle,

In July of 2005, I could honestly say that I was not ready to be your father. I was an ignorant rebellious boy that knew little about life and nothing about parenting. However, I am blessed to be your father. I have learned what responsibility, commitment and being a man is all about. You are beautiful, intelligent and a true reflection of what a great daughter is. If I can help it, you will never need for anything, and it is my endeavor to give you the world. I love you.

To my cousins, Anthony, Adam & Aaron,

You all are truly much more than cousins. We are like brothers. I am proud of all that each of you has accomplished and will accomplish in the future. I am thankful for all of our experiences and I'm grateful to call you family.

Aunt Beverly and Uncle Jesse,

You two are more than an uncle and aunt to me. You're like another set of parents. Coming up, there was little that could stop you two from seeing about me and my siblings. Furthermore, you helped to expose us to so much more. From working in the community to showing us what running a political campaign consists of, I am grateful and I thank you for everything you have done for me. Of course, I couldn't mention you two without mentioning my cousin Justin. Thank you for letting a young little rascal hang with you when I was younger. I'm happy for your future, and I know great things lie ahead for you.

Uncle Andre,

You are one of the biggest influences in my life in helping me to be a respectful and polite gentlemen. You were always tough on me and my siblings when we were coming up, always instructing us on the proper way to speak and conduct ourselves. Those lessons have translated into many doors opening for me. I've learned a lot from you, and am eternally grateful for the many sacrifices you continue to make for our family.

To my in-laws, Marvin & Aletha Darby,

Few people have helped me in the past few years like you two have. You were the first ones to partner with me in my business, allowing me to speak at your businesses, as well as partnering with me in doing my weekly radio show. You have entreated me as a son and have always made me feel welcome. I am forever thankful that you entrusted me in taking your oldest daughter's hand in marriage. I thank you for your ongoing support. To the rest of the family, Priscilla and Patria, thank you for always supporting your big brother.

To Pastor Daniel & Lady Jeannine Grandberry,

You all have been an immense blessing in my life. I don't think you will ever understand the impact that you have had and are continuing to have on me—not just as a man—but as a husband, a father, a preacher and a businessman. You two are great examples of what holiness and unity consist of. Thank you for being there for me and for helping to keep me on course in life. I will forever value your leadership and guidance.

To my Bailey Temple family,

Although I am no longer a member there, BT will always be home to me. It was where I got my start as a minister and so many other great positions. Along with my grandparents, the members, past and present, raised me. You watched me grow from a boy into a man, literally. I will never forget my roots. To the memory of the late Pastor James M. Johnson, thank you for allowing a young man to find his place in ministry. Not too many pastors would have given me a shot.

To my Gordy Memorial family,

It's only been a few years since my wife and I have become members at the church. But from day one, you all have made us feel right at home. I enjoy working side by side with each of you, helping to make our pastor's vision a reality. The Gordy Memorial church family is special, and I am grateful to each of you for your continued love and support.

To Joe "Rock" Fielder,

I hope that you didn't think I would do acknowledgements and not mention you. You were one of the initial people who spoke into my life regarding all of the things that God would do in my life. As you can see, it is all coming to pass. From being in ministry, hosting radio and television programs, to now writing this book, you were right about all of these things. What's amazing to me is that there is much more that you have spoken that is yet coming to pass. I thank God that whenever I need sound advice and wisdom, I can count on you to deliver exactly what God tells you. You are a mentor, true friend and example. I am glad that God placed you in my life.

To my friend and brother, Antoine D. Jackson (Mr. #100WattLife),

This book probably wouldn't have happened without your guidance and assistance. I can always count on you, whether it's a simple question about publishing, to all of the great flyers and promotional pieces you design for me. Thank you. God truly blessed me when He connected us.

To my editor, Tenita Johnson,

You are a true God-send. Your expertise in helping me to make this book possible is beyond the value of money in my opinion. You have taken this book and made it something that I can be truly proud of. I thought I was a good writer before meeting you, but you have shown me that I can be an even better writer. Looking forward to working with you on many more projects in the future.

To all my family and friends,

I appreciate everyone who has ever supported me, came to one of my events, gave me an encouraging word, prayed for and with me, and has been by my side through thick and thin. It's hard to name people, but there are some who I have to mention: Jamar Sumlin (Leila), Tremaine Woods (Brittany), Joseph Williams (Roslyn), and my good friend, Latoddra Butler—you all have literally pushed and encouraged me to this point. I know that I can always count on your support in anything that I do. Without a strong support system, no one can truly be successful. I love you all like family and truly appreciate everything that you have ever done for me.

To my Broom/Ferguson family, The Walker family, and all of the Riley family: Sometimes we only see each other once a year at family functions and reunions. However, no matter how far apart we all may be, or how often or less we see each other, our bonds remain strong. It's a pleasure to have such great family that I can depend on. We are all blessed to have each other. Much love always.

To the host of pastors and preachers who have ever supported me,

Thank you to leaders like Bishop John H. Sheard; Pastor Lavelle Whitaker; the late Admin. Asst. Willie Sheard; Pastor Don W.

Shelby; Pastor David and Lady Derica Sumlin; Pastor Charles Heath; Pastor Randall and Lady Roxanne Greenwood; Pastor Wade K. Smith; Pastor Waverly Bumbrey; Pastor Robert D. Taylor; Apostle Dontez Williams; Elder Wardell Woods; Elder Matthew Gillery; Elder and Missionary McMullan; Elder Ethan Sheard; Elder Kellen Brooks; Elder Cahlyn McCree; Elder Derric Scott; Elder Josiah Jones; Minister Don. W. Shelby III; Minister Kijuan Banks; Minister Reginald Vaughn; and many, many more. You all have, in one way or another, influenced my ministry by your sound wisdom, godly examples and opportunities granted for me to utilize my gifts as God has blessed me.

In memoriam,

Michael and Anita Riley (mentioned in dedication), Minister Ricardo Harris and Mother Maggie Beckon.

Again, there are so many people that I can thank, and lest I forget anyone, I will just leave it here. If you have supported and encouraged me, you know who you are. I pray that I will be able to repay each of you in some way or another. In the meantime, I'll keep doing what so many have believed that I am able to do, and that is continuing to unleash my greatness and doing my part to impact this world. Thank you, and I love you all.

DeAndre M. Riley

ABOUT THE AUTHOR

Everybody has something to say—but not everyone makes an impact with their words. DeAndre Riley, also known as D.R. Speaks, is a multi-faceted force in and out of the four walls of the church. After suffering the loss of both biological parents at a young age, D.R. Speaks made poor decisions that could have destroyed his future. Instead of allowing those things to defeat him, he used them as stepping stones to his unmerited success. As a minister, motivational speaker and author, he seeks to deposit a simple, yet profound principle in the lives of those he may come in contact with: inspire, inform, instruct, and impact.

After his return from college at Michigan State University, D.R. Speaks was immediately thrust into the ministry of his then home church, Bailey Temple Church of God in Christ. Soon after he accepted the call, he was called up and out. While teaching and preaching at various churches throughout the metropolitan Detroit area and surrounding suburbs, he was shaped into a phenomenal orator and servant. It was through his creative ability to dissect the

Word of God and teach others how to apply it to everyday life that he discovered his purpose and passion—helping others lead, grow and serve in their God-given purpose.

As the founder of D.R. Speaks Enterprises, he provides motivational speaking and consulting to ministries, organizations, business professionals and corporations. His sole belief that words are the greatest tool given to mankind to aid them in living the life they are destined to live has opened numerous doors of opportunity. D.R. Speaks can be heard worldwide on his radio show, "I've Got Something to Say." This weekly power-packed show inspires others to press past their failures, embrace the future, dream bigger and reach their full potential—then encourage someone else to do the same.

From being an armor bearer and COGIC District Youth Pastor, to conference host and Assistant Church Administrator at Gordy Memorial COGIC, he's proven that he is not only called, but surely chosen for such a time as this. He currently serves as a licensed and ordained elder in the Church of God in Christ, faithfully working in ministry at Gordy Memorial Church in River Rouge, MI. His wisdom, charisma and knowledge speaks for itself—long before he ever speaks a word. D.R. Speaks currently resides in Lansing, MI with the love of his life, Porsha.

For more information or for booking, please visit **www.drspeaks.org.**

CONTACT AND BOOKING

All booking requests to be sent to: info@drspeaks.org
Website: www.DRspeaks.org

Stay Connected with D.R. Speaks**

Facebook: DeAndre Riley – D.R. Speaks
(Facebook.com/DRileySpeaks)

Twitter: @DRileySpeaks

Instagram: @DRileySpeaks

YouTube: DRspeaks

LinkedIn: www.linkedin.com/in/DRileySpeaks

***Please share your pics and posts about Greatness Unleashed
with your social network, and use the hashtags below. Your
support is greatly appreciated.***

#DRspeaks #GreatnessUnleashed